10 Steps to Happiness

The real reason you're struggling with life, and how to fix it, fast!

By Janine Lattimore

Contents

Introduction

What is the real reason you are struggling with life?
It is the way you see yourself and the world.

One of the biggest lies people believe about themselves is that they are not enough. The main reason why people do not feel content and fulfilled is because they do not truly love themselves. In this book I teach you practical ways to begin to love yourself, and to see yourself and your life in a way that reduces stress and overwhelm. I help you to give yourself permission to take care of your own needs first.

Happiness is a learned practice. True happiness is not something you find outside of yourself; it is something that you cultivate within yourself. It is not determined by experiencing certain conditions in your life, it is determined by how you choose to think and feel within everything that you experience in life. Some people have personality types that make them more naturally optimistic, but happiness in the sense of living life with consistent contentment and confidence is a life skill that can be learned and developed. The goal of this book is to teach you those life skills in a simple, fast and effective way that you can practice daily.

Tony Robbins says the smartest thing he does is refuse to "learn something or make a decision about something valuable without making [him]self do something in the moment that commits [him] to follow through." If you do not take action in the moment, it is likely that a multitude of distractions will come up and you will lose your momentum. This is usually our main problem. It is not that we don't know what to do, it is that we know too much, and our lives are so full of options and distractions. Some of the information in this book may not be new to you. You may know it, but you're not putting it into action consistently, and that is part of the frustration and stress. What I give you in this book is an easily actionable process to put what you know into action, and insight into how to clear mental and emotional blocks that are keeping you from being as happy as you want to be. I will help you clear the overwhelm, and give you a focused path to follow to get to where you want to go: a life that feels good and is working for you.

For this reason, throughout this book I have written *Do It Now Action Points*. These are immediately doable actions that will enable you to take the information you have learned on a Step and integrate it as a practice in your daily life. This is also why this book is designed so that you focus on one step at a time. I don't want to just give you more information. I want to help you to make positive changes in your life. The most effective and sustainable way to do that is to make one small change at a time. With each step you will have one action point to implement that is manageable for everyone. However, if you are an over-achiever like me, I will also give you an option for how you can turbo-boost the basic action step.

The focus of this book is not to try and do everything. It is about learning options, and then implementing and sustaining those practices which work well for you, and which you can easily do on a daily or regular basis. Even if you just pick one practice out of the whole book and do it consistently, it is worth far more than having a lot of theoretical knowledge, but not taking action on it. This stuff works, but it only works when you do it.

Book Features

Do It Now Action Point
Gets you started taking action NOW when your motivation
 energy is highest, and taking an action that you can easily make
part of your daily routine.

Extra Help
Extra help for things that you could get stuck on.

Turbo Boost
Tips to maximise the benefit of the practice; a little extra effort for
magnified results.

Power of 5
Many people feel that if they can only spare 5 or 10 minutes for
themselves then why even bother. I am a great believer that
taking even five minutes for yourself can be significant if you use
it wisely. This is where the *Power of 5* stems from. Throughout
this book I will teach you simple practices that only take about
five minutes to do, but which are very effective for building your
level of happiness. At the end of the book there is a summary of
them all that you can refer back to.

Each step builds on the one before
The Steps outlined in this book are designed to be cumulative. By
this I mean that each Step builds on the one before it. Continue
doing the daily action point for Step 1 as you introduce the daily
action point for Step 2. Continue doing the action points for Steps
1 & 2 as you introduce the action points for Step 3, and so on.
Each action point is designed to be quick and easy to do so you
won't be overloaded, and sometimes the action points will
overlap several steps or will be able to be combined into one daily
action.

Help!

If you need help at any time then feel free to email info@janinelattimore.com.

We have such a tendency to delay our satisfaction; to think, when I lose five pounds . . . when I make a certain amount of money, then I can have joy. Then I'll feel satisfied. And it's all lies. It's never gonna happen if we don't just give ourselves permission to have it now.

Kate Northrup – Entrepreneur and Author

Step 1: The Power of Gratitude

Gratitude is the easiest way to begin to create positive change in your life. It is relatively simple to do, takes very little time and effort, and yet creates significant results.

> *When I started counting my blessings,*
> *my whole life turned around.*
> – Willie Nelson

We can only feel one dominant emotion at a time. Thus, if you decide to generate a feeling of gratitude, then negative feelings such as worry and fear are diminished. In his book *Think and Grow Rich* Napoleon Hill stated that "positive and negative emotions cannot occupy the mind at the same time. One or the other must dominate." Practicing gratitude on a daily basis can rewire your neurochemistry. Our brains become programmed by what we think and feel on a repeated basis. The more you think positive thoughts, and feel positive emotions, the more likely these will become part of your dominant mental programming. Regularly focusing on experiencing gratitude (and other expansive emotions such as love, compassion, appreciation and courage) sensitises your brain to positive experiences, and it will get faster at turning these into lasting inner strengths.

> *The meaning you give events, interactions and outcomes*
> *determines how you feel. By creating a ladder of positive and*

Feeling thankful for the person you currently are and what is already in your life can help you let go of wishing you were someone else and your life was something else. Wishing keeps you stuck in a powerless, victim state.

Establishing a Gratitude Practice

When you wake up in the morning or just before you go to sleep at night, or ideally both, take a few minutes (it only takes a few minutes) to focus on feeling gratitude. Starting your day with a feeling of gratitude puts you in a positive state of mind to step out from. We also gravitate towards what we focus on. Practicing gratitude makes you feel good, and makes it more likely that you will notice other things which make you feel good. It helps you to view life from a positive perspective which reduces your stress levels. Ending your day with gratitude relaxes you before sleep. Instead of lying in bed worrying about what might go wrong, lie in bed reflecting on what is going right.

While you sleep, your subconscious mind ingrains your thoughts and works on solving the day's problems. If you go to sleep focusing on things you don't like, things that didn't work, people that hurt you, and fear that you feel, then you will continue to develop beliefs that cause fear and worry in your life. You will continue to attract all of these negative things. The last few minutes before you sleep is a critical time for you to focus on positive thoughts and what you want in your life. Your subconscious mind will take this information and use it while you sleep. So instead of creating beliefs of fear and worry, you will be focusing your subconscious on finding ways to create your dream life and attracting what you want.

You can simply think about what you are grateful for, or write it in a diary, or work through a list with a partner or your child. You could do it as a family around the dinner table each evening if you want. Many people find that physically writing helps them to stay focused in their thinking. It also activates both kinaesthetic (touch) and visual learning. When you engage multiple physical senses, you activate learning and growth in a more powerful way. Writing also externalises thoughts helping you to view them more objectively, and it provides a record you can look back on.

I have a favourite [guided] meditation that has a section dedicated to acknowledging what I feel grateful for. I also have some favourite yoga routines that incorporate gratitude practice. I have found that since I have begun introducing these practices into my routine at least 3 times a week I tend to think about what I am grateful for throughout the day without prompting so it is becoming more of a habit the more I practice.
It is a useful tool for re- directing negative thought patterns I have been trying to change as well.
- Natasha

Do It Now Action Point (a Power of 5 Practice)

5 Key Gratitudes Practice
Once a day, first thing in the morning or just before you go to sleep, think about or write down one thing you are grateful for, or appreciate about:
1. Something you can see/hear/smell/touch/taste right now

2. Something that you achieved today

3. Yourself

4. Your partner (if you do not have a current partner think about a quality/behaviour you would appreciate in a future partner, or appreciate something about the people you live with)

5. Each of your children (if you have children)

These topics have been specifically selected to get maximum results from your gratitude practice. They target areas in our lives where lack of gratitude is common, and where developing a greater level of appreciation will have multiplied benefits.

Gratitude Key 1: something you can see/hear/smell/touch/taste right now. This directs your focus to the present moment, and into your physical senses which helps to break you out of past and future projections of thought, e.g. regret and worry. It also activates your conscious mind and interrupts your automatic subconscious storylines.

The point of power is always in the present moment.
– Louise Hay

Gratitude Key 2: something you achieved today. This increases your appreciation of yourself and feelings of success and confidence.

Gratitude Key 3: yourself. This also increases your appreciation of yourself. Developing a greater sense of self-love and self-worth are foundational to creating a happy, successful life.

Gratitude Keys 4 and 5: your partner and your children. These keys are about developing greater appreciation for those people closest to us. This strengthens the core relationships in our lives. Often, we criticise those closest to us more than anyone else. We can very easily take them for granted, or get stuck on things about them that irritate us because they are so frequently in our space. Consciously focusing our attention each day on aspects we appreciate about them can shift how we see them and how we relate to them, and create significant positive improvement in the relationship. This in turn reduces stress for everyone involved. The effect of this is even greater if you also aim to express that appreciation to them daily i.e. tell them what you like about them, how they are supporting you and what you think they are doing well.

Extra Help

If you are in a very low emotional place, it can feel challenging to think of things you are grateful for, let alone to actually FEEL grateful. You may feel so stuck in stress, fear, worry and doubt that you can't settle your mind enough to think of anything that you are grateful for. Or, you may struggle because trying to think of things to be grateful for gets you thinking about all the things you feel you don't have, and all the things you lack. Alternatively, you may feel like you need certain things to happen in your life before you can be grateful. It may feel crazy to be thinking of things to feel grateful for when your life feels so far from what you want it to be. However, gratitude is a very effective tool for initiating positive change in your life.

If you are struggling to think of things to feel grateful for, then try using this softened gratitude question: If I could feel grateful for one thing right now, it could be . . .

You can also start with very basic things to be grateful for. For example, you could write down statements like:
"I could feel grateful that I am breathing."
"I could feel grateful that I can read."
"I could feel grateful that I can walk and talk."

"I could feel grateful for the chair I am sitting on"
"I could feel grateful that I am able to laugh."

I had very low self- esteem. So, I started with one thing about myself that I kinda maybe liked a little. Whenever I started with the inner hate dialogue, I'd say "Maybe so, but I do like ... about me", and I would focus on that one thing. Eventually, as I focused on what I liked, I'd see other things I liked.

- Barbara

Another option is to think of someone else who is struggling in life and imagine what they could feel grateful for. Taking a step back from a topic in this way and removing ourselves from the centre of it, can help to open our mind to see things in a different way and think more creatively. Sometimes, when I start thinking of things I am grateful for, I start to feel fearful that I might lose what I have. When this happens, instead of saying "I am grateful for...", I shift to using the reframed phrase: "I like . . . ". "I like" has a lighter, more playful energy to it that shifts me out of the fear of loss, but still sets my focus in a positive direction on what I want more of in my life. I think of gratitude as being thankful for things I have and appreciation as feeling good about the things that I like, love and enjoy. Appreciation feels more uplifting to me, however, I invite you to explore into a way of doing a gratitude practice that feels best to you.

Turbo-Boost

Activated Appreciation.
You can boost the power of your gratitude practice by activating your appreciation. To do this, for each point of gratitude or appreciation you think of, also feel it. Notice what it feels like in your body and use your focus and imagination to increase the

feelings of thankfulness, love, delight and peace. These feelings have a high vibrational energy and are powerful activators for positive change. Feel it in your body, let it become more intense. Dr Rick Hanson describes it as sensing the experience sinking into you, and notes that this is the most effective way to rewire your brain for happiness.

An example of this process might look like this:
Basic appreciation: I am grateful for the bed that I am lying in.

Activated appreciation: I am grateful for how warm and soft this bed feels. I am grateful that I find it comfortable. I am grateful that I have a duvet cover that I love the design of. I appreciate that my bed feels beautiful and inviting to me. I am grateful that I feel like I can relax when I curl up in bed.

Thank you More Please
For each point of gratitude or appreciation that you think about and feel, you can play further and say "Thank you, more please.", which is giving yourself permission to feel and experience more of that, and saying to the divine powers that you are thankful for what you have, and this is what you would like more of in your life.

Thank Someone
Another way to turbo boost practicing gratitude is to thank someone in person, or with a note. You can thank someone who is close to you, or someone who you hardly know who did something you appreciated. You can thank someone for something they did for you in the past or the present. Speaking something, especially when you say it to someone else, adds another level of power to your thoughts.

Gratitude Practice Steps

➤ Take a few minutes when you wake up and/or when you go to bed to work through the 5 Key Gratitudes Practice. If you need to, then use the reframe questions: "If I could feel grateful for one thing right now it could be . . ." or "I like . . ."

➤ Turbo boost your gratitude practice by:
  o Noticing and amplifying feelings of gratitude, appreciation, love and peace

  o Thinking about why you feel grateful and saying "Thank you, more please"

  o Thanking people in your life on a daily basis.

Step 2: Move Your Body – with Pleasure

Physically moving is another easy way to shift energy in yourself. I don't mean take on an intense exercise programme to fix or improve your body. I mean identify a way of being active that you enjoy which you can do on a regular basis. It is best if the activity you engage in is beneficial for you both physically and psychologically. Aim to move in ways that renew you rather than exhaust you.

What you do will depend on what YOU like to do. Some people like the meditative rhythm of running, some people like to dance, some people like going for walks, some people like lifting weights and some people like taking a gym class. Let go of any "should" i.e. what anybody else says you should be doing in terms of exercise. The only necessary requirement is that it be physical activity which makes YOUR body, mind and soul feel good. I'm inviting you to let go of exercising with the goal of getting fit or losing weight (although that may happen as a side effect) and instead to move your body for pleasure. Exercise to feel better physically, for the delight of moving, and out of appreciation for the amazing entity that is your physical body.

Here are the ways moving your body facilitates happiness:
- It boosts your energy levels
- It helps you to fall asleep at night and sleep more soundly

- It helps remove toxins from your body
- It improves brain function
- It increases serotonin production and release (you'll learn why that is beneficial in Step 3)
- It helps release stuck emotional energy and stress
- It stimulates the flow of nourishment (blood) and life-force energy
- It can help bring you out of your mind and into your body and the present moment
- Light to moderate enjoyable movement shifts your nervous system from stress mode to relax and heal mode

Physical Health and Happiness

While there is a strong connection between physical health and happiness, which is why I have included moving your body as a step in this book, they do not equal each other. Many people exercise with the aim of making their body look better because they think they will feel happier if they are slimmer, or have big, toned muscles. Losing weight and having a well sculpted body will not in and of itself make you happy. Happiness is about how you see yourself and life in general. There is no guarantee that if you look good physically that you will then feel good about yourself. This is why many people yoyo diet or get obsessive about exercise, because they are working on their physical body but mentally and emotionally, they have a lot of stress, or resistance or issues with unworthiness that are causing imbalance in their body.

Conversely, you do not need to be physically healthy to be happy. From the end of 2011 to the beginning of 2017, I experienced an extreme amount of stress in my life and became quite ill as a result. At the start of 2017 I decided that I was going to get well and that became my driven focus, until I realised something crucial that became a turning point for me; I did not need to be well to be happy. Consequently, I stopped trying to be physically healed, and focused instead on being happy. I let go of making my happiness conditional on healing my illness.

You do not need to be healthy to be happy. However, you do need to be happy to be healthy. The work of Bruce Lipton and other scientists has clearly shown that our thoughts and feelings influence how our cells function. Our bodies are not driven by our genetics; they are driven by our thoughts. That is why the placebo effect works. Your genes are like a general blueprint for building your body, which genes are expressed, i.e. which parts of the blueprint actually get built, is determined by the environment your cells experience. That environment is influenced by what you think and believe, what you feel, what toxins you are exposed to and how well you are nourished.

Any form of physical activity can have benefits. However, exercising with a sense of forcing yourself, discomfort, boredom, pain, frustration, and self-criticism is quite different to moving with pleasure. Your body thrives when you are feeling good, loving life and loving yourself. People who are in a loving relationship are often said to be "glowing". Love and joy are radiant. It is not being loved that makes people glow, it is that love is flowing in them and you can generate that for yourself.

Exercise and physical activity alone will not make you happy, Happiness is determined by our mental, emotional and energetic state, and when we align a loving joyful emotional state with moving for pleasure, the benefits are vastly multiplied. While this is the ultimate goal, the good news is that if you are not in such a good mental and emotional place yet, physical activity can be a bridge to getting there. I have included exercise, and stimulating the release of our natural feel-good chemicals as Step 2 and 3 of this book, not because they create true happiness, but because they can help you get from a low, unhappy place to a more relaxed positive state where you feel more open to begin dealing with emotions and shifting thought patterns. It is very challenging to go straight from depressed to happy. It is easier to take smaller steps to bring you up. Steps 1-4 of this book give you easy, effective happiness promoting action-points before we get into the more challenging stuff of dealing with uncomfortable and painful emotions and limiting thoughts.

What is Your Activity Challenge Point?

The aim of this step is to help you to move more in an enjoyable way. If you think you already do that well, great, skip ahead to the next chapter. Most people though, have an activity challenge point, which is something about the way they include physical movement in their daily routine that could be tweaked to make it more enjoyable and effective.

Below are 5 common activity challenge points. Which ones do you identify with?
    1. I don't move enough on a daily basis

2. There are frequent times when I am sedentary for extended periods, but I am otherwise active

3. I feel driven to work-out

4. I don't enjoy the exercise I am doing

5. I often experience pain and/or injury from the exercise I am doing

Activity Challenge Point 1: I don't move enough on a regular basis

People usually have this challenge point for one of two reasons: they find movement difficult or painful for health reasons, or they are an exercise-phobe, often because of bad experiences in the past or lack of self-love. Either way, if this is your challenge point, then start with thinking about activities that you like to engage in. For example, you may like walking on the beach, or crazy dancing with your kids, or walking round the shops, or tending a garden. Make a list of any physically mobile activities that you enjoy doing. Now identify one that you can do for at least five minutes on a daily basis. Yes, that's all. Why? Because adding in just one five minute period of enjoyable physical activity each day is doable and sustainable. Moreover, multiple studies have shown that regular engagement in short periods of movement still has significant benefits for your physical and mental wellbeing. You can do more if you want, but doing just one extra five minute activity is a good place to start.

Here are some ideas of activities you could do for 5 minutes each day:

- play an active electronic game like ones where you have to physically hit things or dance

- walk round the block before breakfast

- do a section of trimming or weeding in the garden

- punch a punching bag

- perform a couple of yoga poses

- dance to a song or two

- hula hoop or shoot some hoops

- do 2 or 3 strength-based exercises like push-ups, or bicep curls

- vacuum a room (maybe not quite so enjoyable, but satisfying)

- play chase with your dog or child/children

Activity Challenge Point 2: There are frequent times when I am sedentary for extended periods but I am otherwise active
A fellow group fitness instructor was talking to me once about her smart-watch movement reminder. I was curious as to why she felt she needed one because she taught group fitness classes 6 days a week. She said that while she was very active a lot of the time, there were times during the week when she worked on the computer for 3-4 hours, and would be sitting still for long periods of time. It was for those times that she really needed the reminder to move. If this is your activity challenge point, then you probably experience something similar in your life. You may go for a walk every day, or to an exercise class multiple times a week, but then you are sedentary for long periods during other parts of your day.

If this is the case, what would benefit you is to take regular movement breaks. It is helpful to set some sort of reminder on your smart-watch, phone, or computer to prompt you to get up and move every 50-60 minutes, or even every 25-30 minutes. You do not need to move much. You could stand up and go and get a drink of water, do a few stretches, hula hoop for a few minutes, play an upbeat song and have a dance-break, do a yoga pose, or do a set of push-ups. Do whatever feels good for you.

Activity Challenge Point 3: I feel driven to work-out
Do you feel driven to work-out almost every day? Do you feel guilty if you miss a work-out? Do you force yourself to exercise even when you are sick or the weather is unpleasant? Do you work-out to feel good about yourself? Excessive and overly strenuous exercise, even the contemplation of it, stimulates your sympathetic nervous system (fight or flight response) to activate your adrenal glands and flood your body with adrenaline. Adrenaline is helpful from time to time when we need increased blood flow to our brain and muscles to take action, but consistent high levels of adrenaline in your body can lead to feeling exhausted and unsettled, and experiencing cognitive decline, poor sleep, a compromised immune system, slowed physical healing and issues related to high blood pressure. That's not very conducive to health or happiness.

Take a step back and try to identify why you feel so driven to exercise. Usually, it is because you are trying to earn something, or you are trying to avoid something. One common reason people push themselves to excess in fitness workouts is to feel like they have worked hard; to feel satisfaction about how hard they worked. This stems from conditional thinking i.e. I feel good about myself when I have worked hard (often this is also: if I have worked harder than other people). The problem with this is that it is temporary and conditional. You have to keep working hard in order to keep feeling good about yourself. This type of thinking comes from a belief that we have to earn everything in life: we have to earn respect, we have to earn success, we have to earn love. Underlying that belief is the common root belief: I am not worthy; I am not enough.

An alternative to feeling good about yourself because you've worked hard, is feeling good about yourself because you've done something healthy and right. The belief here is "I am a good person because I do good things". Again, this is conditional thinking, and the problem is that usually if you have this belief, you only feel good about yourself if you keep doing things that you consider to be right and responsible. You link your self-worth to what you do, and if you don't do the right thing or somehow do the wrong thing then you feel like your worthiness is decreased. Here too, the strong underlying belief with this is "I am not enough".

Another common reason people become obsessive about exercise is because it is a way of escaping from dealing with uncomfortable feelings. It is a distraction, but unlike drugs or alcohol it is a worthwhile one. You are doing something good for your health, so you feel good about yourself, but really you are using exercise as a way of escaping from difficult feelings. Exercise can be a very pleasant escape. Not only can you feel worthy about doing something healthy, but when we perform high intensity exercise, we also experience a rush of feel-good chemicals in our bodies – the aptly named "runner's high". I will talk about these natural "happy" chemicals in depth in Step 3. They are not bad. Like exercise in general they can help make it easier for us to develop the thoughts and feelings conducive to true happiness, but they themselves are a conditional and temporary prop. Unless you change your thought patterns, and learn to love and accept yourself deeply, when you stop exercising or finish your workout, then the unresolved emotions and inner criticism that you were trying to get away from will come right back up. I am going to teach you how to resolve and shift these unhelpful emotions and beliefs in Steps 5-8. For now, simply work on awareness. Become aware of what is driving you to exercise, and create one change to make your exercise more about pleasure.

Activity Challenge Point 4: I don't enjoy the exercise I am doing
If you don't like what you are currently doing for exercise, then begin to think about, and look for, physical activities you do enjoy engaging in. If you are taking an exercise class which you are not enjoying, try a different one. Let your pleasure be your guide, not what you think, or someone else says, you should be doing. There is no point in forcing yourself to do exercise you don't like even if it is said to be really good for you. If you are forcing yourself to do it, then doing it will be causing you stress. The stress of doing it will be counteracting the good of the exercise. You will also struggle to stay motivated, and you will feel resistant emotions before, and likely during, the experience. All movement is helpful, so do something you enjoy, and then you get the added health promoting benefits of feeling pleasurable emotions while you do it.

Activity Challenge Point 5: I often experience pain and/or injury from the exercise I am doing.
There is a school of belief that you haven't worked out properly unless it hurts in some way: it's the "no pain, no gain" philosophy. Some people also like the endorphin rush of working out so hard they feel pain. While body builders may enjoy pushing themselves to their limits to achieve a desired result, that is about shaping the body to look a certain way, not about health and happiness. As I noted in Activity Challenge Point 3 above, excessive and overly strenuous exercise, even the contemplation of it, stimulates your sympathetic nervous system (fight or flight response) to activate your adrenal glands and flood your body with adrenaline and consistent high levels of adrenaline can lead to increased anxiety, sleep issues, high blood pressure and increased risk of heart attack and stroke. I believe pain is the body's way of letting you know that what you are doing is harmful, and that you need to stop. It is a sign of stress and a message to be listened to. It is important to be aware of the possible long-term damage which may be caused by consistently pushing your body to a point of pain.

If you are training hard to reach a particular goal, then be very conscious of practicing correct techniques to minimise harm on your body. If you are pushing yourself because you think you need to in order to be fit and healthy, then know that you do not need to do this, and I would recommend reducing your efforts to avoid stress and strain.

Do It Now Action Point

Do the actions that are connected with the Activity Challenge Point or Points that are relevant for you.

Activity Challenge Point 1: Identify an activity you enjoy doing and make a routine time each day to do it for at least 5 minutes.

Activity Challenge Point 2: Set a regular reminder to get up and move every 50-60 or 25-30 minutes during sedentary periods during the day.

Activity Challenge Point 3: Become aware of what is driving you to exercise and create one change to make your exercise more about pleasure.

Activity Challenge Point 4: Begin to think about, and look for, physical activities you do enjoy engaging in. Create one change to make your exercise more about pleasure.

Activity Challenge Point 5: If you want to continue engaging in the exercise you are currently doing then seek help to ensure you are performing actions using correct techniques. Alternatively, begin to think about, and look for, other physical activities you enjoy doing which are gentler on your body, and create one change to make your exercise more about pleasure.

Extra Help

If you have trouble getting or staying motivated to move, then here are some tips to help:

> ➤ ***Attach more movement to something you already do.*** For example, if you go out of the office at lunchtime to buy lunch, then walk round the block before you buy your food, or put some music on when you're getting dinner and shake your booty round the kitchen every night, or do a yoga sun salutation sequence each morning as soon as you get out of bed.

> ➤ ***Get moving with someone else.*** It can be more fun getting active with other people.

> ➤ ***Try something new.*** If you don't enjoy what you are currently doing for exercise or are struggling to think of something you would enjoy doing, then ask what other people do, or search community newsletters and online to see what is on offer in your area, or try an activity that you haven't done before to see if you like it.

Turbo-Boost

Move for pleasure more often

You may want to establish a routine of having an active family outing every Sunday afternoon, or join a new fitness class, or meet up with a friend or two for an explore walk once a week. Ask yourself: how can I have fun being active?

Time your activity for increased benefit
It is best to move most in the morning and during the day. Exercising outside during the morning helps to correctly set your circadian rhythms for sleep at night. This could be a walk before breakfast, or incorporating a 15–20-minute walk into how you get to work, or walking the kids to school.

Long periods of inactivity such as sitting at a desk all day, standing at a counter all day, or spending hours in a car or on a couch causes tension and blockages in our muscles, lymph and connective tissues. This accumulated stress can make us feel restless and uneasy as well as stiff, tense and sore, and consequently unable to relax into sleep. Being active consistently during the day helps us to fall asleep and stay asleep at night. If you spend long blocks of time during the day in a stable or seated position e.g. standing at a counter or seated at a desk, then set a timer to prompt you to move around every 50-60 minutes or so. You do not need to move a lot – walk to the toilet or go get a drink, or do a couple of yoga stretches or find a spare spot and hula hoop for a minute or two or pump some hand-weights.

Avoid doing strenuous exercise within three hours of going to bed (except sex). Vigorous exercise raises your body temperature, and sleep comes more easily when your temperature is decreasing. Engaging in highly stimulating exercise such as a Zumba or spin class within 2-3 hours of going to bed may also make it difficult for you to mentally relax for sleep.

Move Your Body Practice Steps

➢ Identify your Activity Challenge Point.

➢ Move more, or less, or differently according to your Activity Challenge Point.

➢ Think about organising to get active on a regular basis with your partner, children or friend/s to help make it more enjoyable and keep you motivated.

➢ Turbo boost your movement practice by moving more often, or adjusting the time you exercise to the morning or during the day to improve the benefit it gives you.

Step 3: Get Chemical Help

By chemical help I am not talking about drugs – recreational or pharmaceutical. However, if you have a condition such as clinical depression, then prescribed medicines may be an option to help you feel better. What I am referring to in this step are the natural chemicals we produce in our body that make us feel good.

Your body is wired to produce four main feel-good neurotransmitter chemical messengers. As with exercise, the release of these natural chemicals will not transform the root thought patterns that determine how much contentment you feel in life, but they do help you to feel better for a period of time. This makes it easier to then change your negative thought patterns.

These 4 feel good neurotransmitters are:
Serotonin
Dopamine
Endorphins
Nitric Oxide

Serotonin

Serotonin is a chemical produced by your nerve cells which sends signals between cells in your body. It is mostly found in your digestive system, blood, brain and throughout your central nervous system. Serotonin is considered a natural mood stabiliser, and can help reduce depression and regulate anxiety. Will-power and impulse control can also be affected by serotonin levels, and if your serotonin levels are low, you may have difficulty finishing tasks and staying focused. Serotonin also aids with sleep, digestion and bowel function. Blood platelets release serotonin to help heal wounds. Your libido can also be affected by serotonin levels. High levels of serotonin can stimulate an over-active libido, while low levels can cause you to have little sexual desire.

Like everything in our bodies, the key is to focus on maintaining balance. Most people in modern, urban societies have reduced serotonin levels. This is because the main things that cause a reduction in our serotonin levels are prolonged periods of stress, a low nutrient diet, lack of sunlight, ingestion of caffeine, alcohol, nicotine, artificial sweeteners, antidepressants, and some cholesterol lowering medications, and exposure to toxins such as heavy metals, pesticides and recreational drugs. Implementing ways to raise your serotonin levels naturally will help to restore balance to your serotonin levels if they are low, without causing your levels to become too high.

Dopamine

Dopamine levels in your body influence brain functions that affect your mood, sleep, memory, learning and motor control. It is often referred to as the "motivation molecule," because it provides the drive and focus you need to be productive. It is heavily involved with attention span, focus, follow-through, motivation, and the ability to experience pleasure. Low dopamine levels could affect your motivation to be physically active. Balanced dopamine levels may help counteract depression. Nicotine, caffeine, and sugar-laden, fat-filled treats increase dopamine levels in the short term, but over time disrupt the natural dopamine production process resulting in decreased dopamine production in the long-term. Lack of protein in your diet could mean you do not have enough L-tyrosine, which is an amino acid that helps to build dopamine in the body. Some studies have found that people who are obese are more likely to be dopamine deficient.

Endorphins

Endorphins act on the opiate receptors in your brain to reduce your perception of pain and boost pleasure, resulting in a feeling of well-being. They are released in response to pain or stress, and they are also released during other activities, like eating, exercise, and sex. Endorphins are largely responsible for the feeling of "runner's high" that you can experience after a cardio-based workout, and can help you experience a more positive and energised outlook on life. Some studies have shown that endorphins may also help relieve stress and anxiety, and boost feelings of confidence and optimism.

Nitric Oxide

Nitric oxide (NO) is the uber-neurotransmitter that increases and balances the levels of all the others: endorphins, dopamine, serotonin, oxytocin and DMT. NO (not to be confused with the nitrous oxide used in dentistry) is a signalling molecule produced by cells in our brains, blood vessels, and lungs. It is also produced by beneficial bacteria in your mouth. The production of nitric oxide is triggered by laughter, orgasm, and other experiences of pleasure, as well as by eating fruits and vegetables high in antioxidants, exercising and certain types of breathwork (nitric oxide is also at work in the sensation of "runner's high"). Creating and releasing nitric oxide improves your circulation as your blood vessels become wider, softer and more flexible.

The sensation of nitric oxide being released lasts only a few seconds, but it is a wonderful few seconds! It sets off a chain reaction of other feel-good chemicals in the body. You feel a shift in your energy and a delicious sense of relaxation. After its release into your system, nitric oxide signals white blood cells to fight infections and destroy tumours, works with anticoagulants to prevent strokes, reduces cellular inflammation and balances levels of neurotransmitters. Researcher Herbert Benson, M.D., describes nitric oxide as a crucial element in what's known as a "peak experience" of ecstatic flow, and explains that it allows new neural connections to be made in the brain.

Anger, fear and grief deplete nitric oxide. If the endothelial lining of your blood vessels has been damaged by free radical molecules created by stress and physical toxins, your body can't release enough nitric oxide to actually reduce free radical activity and tissue damage. However, the nitric oxide mechanism is a positive feedback loop. The more nitric oxide you create, the easier it is for your body to create more. In other words:

Pleasure leads to more pleasure.
- Christiane Northrup

How to Increase Your Feel-Good Chemicals

Here are some simple, fast, and effective ways to increase your serotonin, dopamine, endorphin and nitric oxide levels. I have also summarised these into an infographic which you can save to your phone, or print off and put somewhere you can look at it daily. Many of these activities can be incorporated into what you already do routinely on a daily basis e.g. play music while you get dinner, or hug your partner when you greet them. Others can be Power of 5 activities, and engaging in them for even five minutes will have a significant positive effect.

Laugh Freely (Power of 5)

Whether you laugh for real, or perform acted laughter, your body responds the same way. You could watch or listen to comedy, go to a laughter yoga class, play the *Try Not to Laugh* game, or watch funny animal videos.

Increases: nitric oxide, endorphins

Remember Times of Happiness (Power of 5)

Recalling positive events that have happened in your life increases serotonin production. Practicing gratitude can have the same effect. As the opposite is also true in that remembering sad events can decrease serotonin production, remembering happy experiences and practicing gratitude has the two-fold effect of increasing serotonin production and also keeping you from thinking about unhappy experiences. Remember, "positive and negative emotions cannot occupy the mind at the same time. One or the other must dominate." (Napoleon Hill)

When your mood is low it can be hard to remember happier times. One of the biggest problems in major depression is that people can't recall being happy, and only remember being depressed. If this is the case it can help to talk to a long-term friend and recall happy memories together, or look at photographs or videos of happy events from your past.

Increases: serotonin

Move Your Body Regularly (Power of 5)

Moderate to vigorous exercise can release endorphins and nitric oxide, increase your levels of dopamine and boost serotonin in your brain. The more active you are the more serotonin you have available in your system. Exercise can be as effective, or even more effective, at increasing available serotonin as serotonin-enhancing medications.

Increases: serotonin, dopamine, endorphins, nitric oxide.

Spend Time Outdoors

When you are exposed to sunlight it increases your number of dopamine receptors. It also stimulates the production of vitamin D which increases your serotonin levels, and activates the release of dopamine. Receiving bright sunlight through your eyes also triggers dopamine release and increases serotonin activity. Spend as much time in natural day-light as you can, but be sensible about your sun exposure and avoid sunburn. You receive the most positive mood-lifting effects from exposure to sunlight when you spend time outside early in the morning. To increase your exposure to natural light and sunshine you could go for a 20-minute walk along the beach, or sit outside to enjoy lunch, or take your kids to the park, or hang your washing on the line instead of putting it in the dryer, or have a walking meeting outside.

Increases: serotonin, dopamine

Get in Touch with Others (Power of 5)

Healthy and safe human contact triggers dopamine and serotonin production and the release of endorphins. You could give or receive a massage, caress your significant other, or hug your kids. Even shaking hands with people triggers dopamine production. Petting animals also increases your dopamine and serotonin levels.

Increases: dopamine, serotonin, endorphins

Engage in Sexual Pleasure

Having sex, and experiencing sexual orgasm can give you a boost of nitric oxide, endorphins and serotonin. Anticipation of sex can also stimulate the release of dopamine.

Increases: nitric oxide, serotonin, endorphins, dopamine

Get Quality Sleep

Lack of sleep reduces the number of your dopamine receptors.

Increases: dopamine

Meditate (Power of 5)

Meditation increases dopamine leading to improved focus and concentration. It can also increase your serotonin levels, and stimulate the release of endorphins and nitric oxide, along with calming GABA (gamma aminobutyric acid). Certain breathwork practices, especially those with breath holding, also stimulate increased levels of nitric oxide.

Increases: dopamine, endorphins, nitric oxide, serotonin

Listen to Music (Power of 5)

Listening to uplifting music you enjoy stimulates the release of dopamine and endorphins. Both listening to, and playing music, can modulate your serotonin levels.

Increases: dopamine, endorphins, serotonin

Discover Something New

We are chemically wired to get excited about new things. Dopamine production is triggered when we find something new and exciting in front of us. It is released in anticipation of rewards, especially where the reward is uncertain.

Increases: dopamine

Get in Creative Flow

Dance, sing, paint, knit, create patchwork, make models or jam on a guitar. Getting in a creative flow releases nitric oxide and endorphins, and stimulates dopamine utilisation.

Increases: nitric oxide, endorphins, dopamine

Do It Now Action Point

Pick one of the listed activities that stimulate the release of natural feel-good chemicals and incorporate it into your daily routine somehow. Making it part of your daily routine helps it to become a habit and a regular aspect of your life. Linking it to something that you already do routinely every day is the easiest way to establish a new habit.

Extra Help

Here are some suggestions of quick, easy, doable ways you can incorporate some of the activities listed above into your daily routine:

- Put on your favourite music and dance while you are preparing dinner
- Hug/cuddle someone you love

- Play with your kids seeing who can make the others laugh (crazy laughs and crazy faces are guaranteed to stimulate belly laughter)

- Listen to a short, guided breathwork meditation when you get up in the morning.

- Listen to instrumental music when you are working on the computer or studying.

- Create a routine to be in bed going to sleep by 10:30pm (or earlier)

Turbo-Boost

Two of the most effective ways to increase and balance your levels of feel-good neurotransmitters is through physical activity and meditation. Aim to practice one, or both, of these every day in some way.

You can also turbo-boost this step by combining activities that produce feel good chemicals. For example:

- Listen to music you enjoy while you are exercising (physical activity + listening to music)

- Have active sex with a partner (physical activity + sex + affectionate touch)

- Meditate while listening to music (meditation + listening to music)

- Be physically active outdoors (physical activity + natural light exposure)

➢ Meditate outside by sitting quietly and observing nature, or doing a walking meditation focusing on your breath (meditation + natural light exposure + physical activity).

Get Chemical Help Practice Steps

1. Identify one activity you enjoy doing which raises your feel-good chemical levels and incorporate it into your daily routine – remember, even doing it for five minutes a day is beneficial.

2. Turbo boost your practice by engaging daily in super feel-good chemical activities like meditation or exercise, or by doing things which combine a number of actions which increase your positive neurotransmitter levels.

Step 4: Do More of What You Love

You have likely heard the phrase "do more of what you love" or its counterpart "follow your bliss" many times, and seen it on wall prints, mugs and social media quotes. It is one of those pearls of wisdom that has become so common that we often don't register it any more. Yet it is key to happiness. It is also key to living your purpose. It seems like a simple, obvious thing; if you want to be happy just do more things that you enjoy. In reality, the doing isn't that simple though. There are three main blocks to us not doing what we love:

- ➢ We think we are not allowed to do what we want
- ➢ We think we don't have time to do things just for pleasure
- ➢ We have been living a responsible life for so long that we are not even sure what our bliss is

Don't Be Selfish: Bliss versus Service

There is a dominant belief in western society (and any society with Christian heritage) that we need to serve others to be a good person and that it is more important to be a good person than to be happy. Happiness is often equated with selfishness. Pleasing yourself is often judged as immoral. I am not going to argue whether this belief is right or wrong because it is often tied to people's religious beliefs. However, I would like to raise awareness of it and offer some alternative ideas.

Following your bliss and serving others are often viewed as being separate, even opposing things, as being self-centred versus being self-less. Service is often equated with self-sacrifice, and self-sacrifice is often seen as necessary in order to help others. This is a belief not a fact. It is one point of view that has been perpetuated by many. I think it is very important to look at HOW we are serving others and to open our definition of what service is. Instead of using the word service, let's use the word uplift. What most people desire is not just to help other people but to uplift them, so that they can feel better and be happier. You can't give what you don't have. If you serve people from a place of poverty, then you will not be able to uplift them as much as when you serve them from a place of abundance. The best way to help others, is to bring yourself into a place of richness first so that you have more to give.

When I talk about abundance and richness, I am not just meaning financial assets, although that is good too. I am mainly meaning energy assets and how resourced you feel. If you would like to help other people to feel better and happier, then the best way to do that is to be experiencing a lot of joy for yourself. You radiate what you are feeling and the people around you receive that. Following your bliss is the best way to uplift others. Bliss and service are not separate, they are closely intertwined.

Your bliss serves others.
Your passion is your purpose.

We cannot be self-less and why would you want to be? You are here as a one-of-a-kind creation to live your unique life. No one else will ever exist like you and no one will ever be able to live the life that you are living now. I believe that is a divine gift.

Many people go looking for their purpose in serving others in some way. I'm not saying that is not worthwhile, however, I would argue that your joy is your purpose. When you are lit up, you shine light into the world. So do what lights you up, whatever that may be. It doesn't have to be some grand achievement, it could be crocheting beanies, it could be grooming animals, it could be playing the tuba, or it could be sharing information with large audiences. It doesn't matter what it is. When you do what you love, and feel joy, satisfaction and fun doing it, then that creates an uplifting energy in the world. It creates lightness and a focus on what feels good, as opposed to feeling heaviness when focusing on how to solve other people's problems. Often the best way to solve an issue, is to just have fun and forget about it. Sometimes, when you take your attention off a problem and stop giving it energy then it resolves itself, or you realise it actually doesn't matter that much. Moreover, having fun, relaxes your nervous system and opens you to see and think of more options and solutions.

Most of the time we need to give ourselves permission to do more of what we love and have more fun. The main person limiting you is you. It is usually not what other people are saying or doing, it is what you are afraid they will say or do. That is understandable and normal. Human beings developed as social, tribal beings where rejection from the tribe was practically a death sentence because you were unlikely to survive on your own. Our bodies and nervous systems still carry that imprinting and belief. Being accepted by people and belonging to a group are still two of the strongest motivating factors for humans. However, we live in a big global world of abundant resources now. We have far more capacity to make independent choices and be authentic to ourselves. If you wait for someone else to give you permission to live your bliss, then you might be waiting until your deathbed, because the reality is that we are all living life from our own perspective bubble and we cannot live it any other way. Speaking of deathbeds, the most common regrets listed by

Bronnie Ware in her book *The Top Five Regrets of the Dying"* are:

"I wish I'd had the courage to live a life true to myself, not the life others expected of me."
"I wish I hadn't worked so hard."
"I wish I'd had the courage to express my feelings."
"I wish I had stayed in touch with my friends."
"I wish I had let myself be happier"

Make the decision that you deserve abundant joy, and often it needs to be a decision for yourself. It needs the power of deciding, the power of conscious choosing, because there are a lot of forces around you and within you that will give you the message that you are not allowed to be happy, or happier than others.

Reframing Time

People often say that they don't do what they love because they don't have time. The issue isn't really lack of time. It is about what you are prioritising doing. If you were to look at a typical week and assess what you do regularly and how much time you spend on it, then what would it show you are living your life for? What you spend the most time on is what you are trading your life for. It is what you are making most important. Therefore, the question to ask yourself is, are you giving your time, your life, to what is truly most important to you? If you want some help with reframing what you are giving your time and energy to, then my book *The Great Life Planner* provides a lot of information and an easy system for doing that.

One helpful shift that you can make right now is to reframe the words "time spent" to "time invested". The word spent has a connotation of loss to it. When you spend your money, you don't have it anymore. When you invest your money, then it is working for you and giving you a growth return. Do you want to just spend your time on things where you have no return, or invest your time in things where you do? When thinking about what to do in your day or whether or not to do an activity you could ask: is this worth investing my time in? Nourishing and resourcing yourself is an investment of time, and doing what you love nourishes and resources you.

Asking these types of questions can begin to help you see where you are giving your time to things that are not really important to you and guide you to create time for things that uplift you. Just as it is a worthy thing to uplift others, it is also a worthy thing to uplift ourselves so that we radiate more joy and love.

If reading the last few paragraphs stimulated a feeling of anxiety, resistance or contraction in you then it is likely the reason that you think you don't have time to do things that you enjoy or to relax is because your nervous system is stressed and dysregulated. When your stress bucket is full, the thought of taking on new information or activities or making a change in your life feels overwhelming and your body will resist it. Your nervous system's primary objective is to keep you safe and what is familiar feels safe even if it doesn't feel good. Your body also strives to conserve energy and it takes energy to change your thought and behaviour patterns. If you think that you don't have time for self-care then it is even more important for you to invest time in rest and pleasure because it is likely that you are in a highly stressed state. When we are in a dysregulated state, it feels real that we don't have time because it gives us a sense of everything being urgent which is a hyper nervous system response.

Remember, self-care practices do not need to take long. Consciously engaging in a practice regularly for just five to ten minutes can have a noticeable effect. When the reasons why you can't take time for your wellbeing and pleasure come up, take a slow deep breath, notice what is going on in your body, let your nervous system know it is okay, and make a conscious decision to do what is most important to you (I'll give you some more tools for soothing your nervous system in the next two chapters). Once you start investing time into doing more of what you enjoy you may find that other things start to fall into place both in terms of things that you have been trying to do and in terms of how you value yourself, because you are addressing the root of the issue which is stress in your body.

*It takes the same amount of time to service your wellbeing
as it does to service your stress
– which would you rather invest in?*

How to Identify What You Love

Many adults have become so immersed in responsibility that they struggle to even think of what they enjoy doing any more. Does the question, "What do you do for fun?" leave you struggling for an answer? If you find it difficult to come up with a list of things you enjoy doing, then below are some questions and practices that will help you identify your "pleasure list".

What are the things you think about doing "someday" when you have time/the kids are grown/you retire etc?

Play the "I like" game.
The key word here is "play". Go into a place of limitless possibility in your imagination and adopt an attitude of curiosity. Let go of judgement, being sensible, and any concept of whether you can or cannot do or have it. Now think of things you like. Anything. Have fun with it.

What did you enjoy doing when you were a child?

Try something new.
Is a friend or family member doing something you find interesting? Give it a try yourself. Is there something you've always wanted to have a go at doing? Make the decision to give it a go.

Do It Now Action Point

Use the questions and practices listed under "How to Identify What You Love" to make a list of things you enjoy doing. Your "pleasure list".

Pick one of the things on your list and ask yourself: "How can I incorporate this into my daily life in some way?" You do not have to do it every day, but work on establishing a regular routine of some sort. For example, you may book into a new weekly class, or arrange with a friend to go for a walk together every Tuesday and Thursday morning.

Extra Help

How do I fit all this into my life?
If you are feeling anxious about how to fit another thing into your busy life remember that there are points of crossover with the practices I describe in this book. For instance, playing the "I like' game (in the section: "How to Identify What You Love") can be done as a gratitude practice as it turns your focus to positive thoughts and emotions in the same way that appreciation does. You can also use it to practice sustaining pleasure which helps to rewire your brain to overcome fear. Trying something new can stimulate the production of the feel-good neurotransmitter dopamine, and help you to overcome both fear of failure and fear of the unknown.

I don't feel like it is right for me to take time for myself

If you get stuck with giving yourself permission to do more of what you love, you could try using the Trigger Body Love practice described in Step 6. For example:

> "I love myself for feeling like I am not allowed to take time for myself"

> "I love myself for feeling irresponsible if I get someone else to take care of my children while I go and do something for my own pleasure"

> "I love myself for feeling like my happiness doesn't matter"

Offer yourself acceptance for whatever you are feeling. Acceptance creates space for transformation.

Turbo-Boost

Do more, of more of what you love!
You can do more on a regular basis, or plan something extra special to look forward to.

Do More of What You Love Practice Steps

1. Use the questions and practices listed under "How to Identify What You Love" and make a list of things you enjoy doing.

2. Pick one and ask yourself: "How can I incorporate this into my daily life in some way?" Remember, you can look for

ways that the practices of this book cross-over between steps and achieve multiple results. Choose one or two of these that suit what you enjoy doing and what you want to achieve, and just do those.

3. If you feel uncomfortable doing things for your own pleasure, then use the Trigger Body Love practice from Step 6 to create space for those beliefs to shift and expand.

4. Turbo boost this practice by doing even more of what you love

Step 5: Understand Fear

Fear can help you survive, but more commonly in modern society, it limits and binds us because what we fear is largely in our head. How do we overcome fear when it doesn't serve us? The first step to overcoming fear is to understand what it is. Fear is our sub-conscious mind trying to protect us.

Human brains have a negativity bias. Our brains are wired to more readily notice and remember threats and danger. It is a survival instinct. This was very helpful when humans lived in largely unprotected, predator and hazard rich environments. In our relatively safe modern lives, though, it can become a limitation. Our negativity bias is the reason why we can easily recall bad experiences and negative comments, but may not even register compliments. It is also the reason we prefer to avoid losses over acquiring gains; we would rather hold onto whatever we have even if it is unsatisfactory in some way, than take risks to get more. This can help to keep us safe. Most of the threats and dangers we focus on now though, are ones that we create in our mind, and our mind is often working from incorrect or out-dated data stored deep in its subconscious hard-drive files. This data is mainly based around our parents' beliefs, the messages we received from adults when we were children, the conclusions we drew as children about the experiences we had, and repeated patterns of thinking and behaviour. Consequently, our subconscious emotional mind has a tendency to over-react, or react in a way that doesn't serve us now.

Having an awareness and understanding that our brains natural survival instinct is to focus on what could go wrong and how we could be hurt, is the first big step to effectively managing fear. You can begin to see your fear-mongering subconscious as a big friendly monster trying to protect you. Alternatively, you can see fear as your bodyguard. Bodyguards are strong and intimidating, but they are on your side. They have your back. They are there to protect you. Sometimes, we just need to help them chill out, or give them some up-to-date information that serves us for them to work from.

How to Rewire Your Brain

You can re-wire your brain to overcome this negativity bias. Our brains are pliable and we are able to create new neural pathways throughout our life. One thing to be aware of though, is that our subconscious mind is very resistant to change because what is unfamiliar is viewed through our survival negativity bias as unsafe. This is actually the source of a lot of fear that we experience and this is increased in modern society with its rapid rate of technological, information and culture change. It is also energetically expensive (takes a lot of energy) for your body to do the work of undoing current neural pathways and creating new ones. If you are already experiencing a high degree of stress, your body becomes even more resistant to change and new information.

This is why the first four steps of this book are focused on easier physical action-based things that you can do to begin to reduce the amount of stress you are feeling, because you can only create significant change in your life when you feel relaxed and safe. Learning how to make friends with fear and soothe and regulate your nervous system is incredibly beneficial because everything you desire to do, be or have that you don't already, requires change.

Three Key Ways to Feel Safe and Relaxed and Overcome Fear:
1. Be Present

2. Sustain Pleasure

3. Play Positively with Imagination

Be Present

Regularly bringing all of your focus to the present moment can lead to increased gyrification which is the formation of more folds in the prefrontal cortex of your brain. The prefrontal cortex is the part of your brain associated with higher executive functions like your ability to think flexibly and creatively, switch between tasks and make reasonable decisions. Being present moves you into operating from your conscious mind. When you operate out of your conscious mind you are not working from your subconscious auto-pilot thinking patterns. In other words, being present and conscious in your thinking helps you to override your negativity bias. When you are present in the now moment and that moment is safe, you can feel into a sense of *being* safe, which creates an experience of safety for your body. It teaches your body that it can feel safe and how to feel safe. Additionally, focusing solely on things like the one task that you are doing right now, or the person who is directly in front of you, or what you are experiencing with your physical senses in the present moment, clears mental clutter and over-stimulation and helps your nervous system to relax.

Seated meditation and breathwork is one way to be consciously focused on the present moment. Another, is to direct your conscious focus to anything you are doing e.g. washing dishes, cleaning the car, or walking, and be fully in the sensory experience of it. Notice the movements of your body, smells, sounds, tastes, details you can see and sensations within your body as you engage in a task. Conscious movement practices such as yoga, Tai Chi and somatic movement can also facilitate presence, as can creative activities such as painting and playing music. Being with someone is another opportunity to be present. You can pay attention to things like what they are saying, the pace and volume of their words, their body language, and the movements and changes of colour in their face. You may be amazed at how much more you receive from the conversation when you do this, and how it increases the quality of communication between you.

Sustain Pleasure (a Power of 5 practice)

Remember from Step 1: The Power of Gratitude, that our brains become programmed by what we think and feel on a repeated basis. The more you think positive thoughts, and feel positive emotions, the more likely these will become part of your dominant mental programming. Regularly focusing on experiencing high vibration emotions such as gratitude, love, compassion, appreciation and peace sensitises your brain to positive experiences and makes them feel more familiar and safer. You can rewire your brain to notice and hold onto positive experiences more readily by doing what Rick Hanson, Ph.D. calls allowing good facts to become good experiences, or, "taking in the good". This involves consciously recognizing the good events and experiences of your daily life. These might be relatively minor and ordinary such as getting a good car-park, opening a door for someone who has their arms full, finishing a task by the deadline, watching a funny movie, or hearing a bird sing. Then, when you recognise these uplifting experiences, take 20-30 seconds to sink into the good feeling of them. Instead of just letting them become the dross of life, be present, and allow good feelings to grow in response to them. As Rick Hanson says, "*let the good affect you.*" Aim to do this at least 5-10 times a day. You can notice good things, or good feelings you are currently experiencing, or remember positive events of the past. Even if something feels only a little bit better, what you focus on grows so notice it, acknowledge it, talk about it, and lean into it.

Play Positively with Imagination
(a Power of 5 Practice)

The majority of people are more inclined to use their imagination to create fear rather than manage it. The human mind is a wonderful and powerful thing, and we can use it to serve us, or allow it to run on negative auto-pilot. Brendon Burchard has said that "fear is just usually poor management of our mind."

Here are two ways you can use the power of imagination to overcome fear:

Talk to your fear. When you visualise fear as a big, friendly monster or a bodyguard it helps you to disconnect from it emotionally, and to see it more objectively. You can then look at whether this fear is operating in a way that serves you, or is over-reacting. Sometimes I imagine talking to my fear bodyguard and saying "Thank you for trying to protect me, but I'm okay. It's safe. You can stand down."

Use 'What If' Positively. Generally, we use the question of "what if" in a negative way that creates fear. Our negativity bias search for threats and danger kicks in and we wonder about all the things that could go wrong. There are two ways to approach this. It is wise to be prepared for possible negative situations, but only those that are probable, and which we can have control over. Therefore, the first way to approach using the question of "what if" proactively is to explore the negative possibility fully in light of the questions "Is it probable?" and, "Do I have any control over this?". If the answer to either question is no, then you can thank your fear bodyguard for its concern, but let it know that this is not something you need to be concerned with; it is not being helpful.

The second way to use "What if" proactively is to use it to imagine positive outcomes. What if you were as prepared for good things to happen as you were for bad things to happen? Be light and playful with this. Let go of any need for your positive "what ifs" to be realistic. This is not about actual events; this is about wiring your brain to be more open to positive experiences. You can use this practice to feel sustained pleasure. Imagine a wonderful outcome and feel into it. Your body reacts the same way to imagined experiences as it does to physical experiences. Use that positively.

If using the statement "what if" feels a little heavy because it's like wishful thinking, then try using the statement starter "I like" or "I would like it if" instead. I also like to play with phrasing my desires through the day as "wouldn't it be nice if [insert thing I would like to happen]

Turn fear into fascination

Practice Facilitates Familiarity

When you are in a safe and relaxed state, then you can help your brain to become more flexible and resilient by learning new information and practicing new skills. It is helpful to adopt a growth mind-set as opposed to a fixed mind-set. A fixed mind-set believes that skills and abilities are innate, and avoids trying new things out of fear of failure. A growth mind-set sees all everyday problems and experiences as opportunities to embrace and learn through. Developing a growth mind-set where you are open to trying new things helps you to overcome both fear of failure and fear of the unknown. The more you try new things the more confident you become about managing change in your life.

You can start with trying new things that are relatively safe and use the positive experience from that to move on to trying things with greater and greater challenge and risk involved. This programs your brain with the belief that you are able to learn what you need to cope with new situations.

Do It Now Action Point

Choose one of the practices for creating safety and relaxation to facilitate rewiring your brain to overcome fear, and focus on putting it into action over the next week.

1. Be Present
2. Sustain Pleasure
3. Play Positively with Imagination

Extra Help

Be aware that many of the practices from this step link into, or are a repetition of, practices from the previous three steps of this book. For this reason, you can either choose to continue with a practice you are already doing, or add in a new one. For example, if you are already focusing on establishing a meditation practice in your daily routine, then you may continue with that and simply deepen it with the information about being present. Or, if you feel it is doable for you, then you may wish to add a new practice from this step.

Turbo-Boost

Practice sustaining pleasure just before you go to sleep. The time just before you go to sleep is the most important time for you to focus on positive thoughts and what you want in your life. Your brain is particularly receptive to new learning at this time, and your subconscious mind will take this information and process it while you sleep. Remember, you can link this in with your gratitude practice.

Engage in super practices.   Super-practices are those that have multiple benefits. They are the ones that keep coming up on the action lists for each step. Examples are:

- *Yoga, Tai chi, somatic movement* = exercise + meditative focus + move your body + feel good chemicals and rewire your brain. Turbo boost this further by doing them outdoors.

- *Meditation/being present* = feel good chemicals and rewire your brain.

- *Try something new* = feel good chemicals and rewire your brain. Turbo boost this by making the new thing you try meditation or a conscious movement exercise.

Understand Fear Practice Steps

1. Choose one of the practices for creating safety and relaxation to facilitate rewiring your brain to overcome fear, and focus on putting it into action over the next week.

2. Link the practice in this step into something you are already doing or add in a new practice.

3. Turbo boost rewiring your brain by practicing sustaining pleasure just before you go to sleep or engaging in super practices that have multiple benefits.

Step 6: Accept Your Feelings

Expressing our feelings is a necessity for a happy life
Bronnie Ware – The Top Five Regrets of the Dying

A strong sense of self-love and self-worth are key to happiness and creating a life that feels good and works for you. Without this foundation you can be doing lots of good things on the surface, but inside, you will still feel an emptiness, somehow out of sync and unhappy. Doing "happiness" activities without having a foundation of self-love is like trying to complete tasks in a dimly lit room. You can do them and achieve some results, but it's challenging to put all the pieces together and create flow. Developing strong self-love is like turning on a bright overhead light. It enables you to see everything with much greater clarity, and you can put the pieces together with ease and confidence. If you do not love yourself, then you are holding yourself apart from who you really are, and you are not open to fully receive positive energy. You are in a place of resistance.

Developing self-love is a life-long journey and a day by day, moment by moment choice. The topic of how to learn to love yourself fills books. What I am going to share with you in this Step is a Power of 5 self-love practice that I have found to be extremely effective in helping me to accept and love myself. This practice is based around accepting your feelings, and loving yourself for however you feel. When we acknowledge and accept our feelings, we show love to an essential part of our authentic selves.

What are Feelings?

Emotions are complex. They can be stimulated by sensory experience or by cognitive thinking, or a combination of both. When an emotion is stimulated it triggers a cascade of responses in your body, some chemical, for example the release of stress hormones or feel-good neurotransmitters; and some physical, such as increased heart rate, perspiration or muscle response. One theory is that the primal role of emotions was to motivate adaptive behaviours that helped us to survive.

Good and Bad Feelings

Personally, I do not like defining emotions as good or bad, or even positive and negative. I believe that all feelings are valid and serve us in some way. Like Dr Joan Rosenberg, creator of Emotional Mastery, I define emotions as either pleasant or unpleasant, or, comfortable or uncomfortable. Pleasant/comfortable feelings are the ones which make us feel good, for example, love, peace, joy, excitement, fun, happiness, bliss, connection, acceptance, strength and confidence. Unpleasant/uncomfortable feelings are the ones we often try to avoid, or suppress, or think we shouldn't feel, or believe are sinful in some way, or see as harmful. These are feelings like anger, sadness, hurt, pain, grief, guilt, loss, fear, envy, despair and shame.

Abraham Hicks defines pleasant feelings as those we feel when we are aligned with the truth of who we are, and unpleasant feelings as an indicator that we are thinking something that our higher self knows to be untrue. I like this definition as it supports the concept that all feelings are messages for us. They tell us something about our needs and our thought patterns.

Mastin Kipp - Claim Your Power

Fear of Unpleasant Emotions

Many people are afraid to feel unpleasant emotions and will go to great lengths to avoid feeling them. We can be afraid that if we let the feeling start then it won't stop, or that the emotion will be too intense and overwhelm us, or that we'll lose control somehow. However, the more you fight an emotion the stronger it will become; what we resist, persists. We can resist our feelings by trying to physically shut them down through tensing our muscles, holding our breath or swallowing hard. People can also resist their feelings by trying to analyse or fix them, by projecting or blaming them on circumstances or others, or by distracting themselves with food, alcohol, drugs, sex, shopping, or social media.

German Proverb

Remember the human negativity bias we talked about in Step 5? Human beings have become very adept at using their minds to imagine worse case scenarios. We can overcome this fear with understanding. Both understanding how emotions work, and approaching our emotions with an attitude of acceptance and curiosity. Unpleasant emotions do not feel good or safe. Consequently, avoiding them is a learned survival response. It's the same as learning not to put your hand on the stove when it is on once you have been burned by a hot element. However, when it comes to feelings, avoiding feeling the unpleasant feelings we experience can be more harmful than expressing them; our fear of feeling an unpleasant emotion usually becomes a far greater uncomfortable feeling than the one we fear to feel.

When you find a quiet, safe space and allow a feeling to fully rise within you, then it will flow through you quite quickly. If you haven't tried this before you may be surprised at how fast a feeling comes and goes when it is freely expressed. Unpleasant feelings usually feel like they are bigger and stronger because we grow them, either with negative thoughts, or by resisting them which essentially creates a dam of building stress. It can help to see unpleasant feelings as a message and ask, "What is this feeling showing me?" Unpleasant feelings are usually an indicator that a need you have is not being met somehow, therefore another helpful question can be, "What do I need that I am not receiving?"

Our experience of feeling capable in the world, of experiencing emotional strength, is directly tied to our capacity to both experience and move through those unpleasant feelings.
- Dr Joan Rosenberg

Acceptance is the key to creating change. You don't have to try and force your thoughts or feelings to be something they are not. You do not have to change or fix yourself before you can love yourself. When you love yourself for however you are feeling as you are now, you are saying it is okay for you to be who you are. You don't NEED to change, but through this process transformation can happen naturally and effortlessly.

One of the fundamental laws of change seems to be that things need space in order to change. They need room around them in order to find new form.
- Gay Hendricks – Learning to Love Yourself

Acceptance opens up flow in your body, mind and emotions. The practice described in this step is about accepting your feelings as they are. Accepting that they are what they are. You do not need to try and work out why you feel that way, simply accept that you do, and allow the feeling to be expressed. Acceptance in this sense is not just giving up, or saying that your uncomfortable or painful experience was okay. It is accepting the feeling you have within your body, and giving it space to express and move so that it can be transformed or released.

This self-love exercise also develops your awareness of your authentic self. It helps you to become aware of what you truly think and feel, and therefore who you truly are, and it does so from a place of non-judgemental acceptance. When you feel like you do not need to hide your feelings from yourself, and move into more consciously knowing how you think and feel, you begin to feel more confident, and live more deliberately. You act from the knowledge of who you are rather than unconsciously responding to what others want.

3 Part Self-Love Practice - Trigger Body Love

The following practice is based on that taught by Gay Hendricks in his book *Learning to Love Yourself* (which I highly recommend). It also correlates with Joan Rosenberg's emotional reset formula. You can use this process to "take in the good" and sustain pleasure as we discussed in Step 4, or you can use it to accept and release uncomfortable emotions. Through this practice you are offering yourself acceptance for whatever you are feeling, without judgement, and giving your feelings space to be. When you acknowledge and allow your feelings to flow freely, they generally do not last for longer than 90 seconds and dissipate completely. Ignoring your feelings, or resisting them by thinking that it is somehow wrong to be feeling what you are feeling, or to avoid your feelings because you are scared they might be too powerful to deal with, causes them to stay stuck as an energy in your body.

Part 1. Identify a Trigger

The easiest way to learn to do this practice is to set aside 5 or 10 minutes in a quiet place where you won't be interrupted and perform it like a conscious meditation. Once you learn how to do it you can begin to perform it in the midst of your daily life and feel empowered to stay fully present to all of your feelings.

The first part of this process is to identify an emotional trigger, which is something you feel an emotional response to. Possible triggers for this practice could be:

> ➢ Sensing into a general feeling you are feeling in this moment

> ➢ Thinking of a significant person in your life and exploring what you feel when you think of them

> ➢ Thinking of a situation in your life that you don't want

> ➢ Remembering a painful experience

I recommend trying the first two triggers before starting to use this practice to process stronger uncomfortable feelings. Another trigger I have used from time to time is to sit quietly and focus on a part of my body, ask myself how I feel about that part of my body, and then love myself for whatever sensations or emotions come up.

Dr Joan Rosenberg

Part 2. Feel the Emotion in Your Body

Once you have identified an emotional trigger to focus on, feel into any sensations in your body. What we feel emotionally is felt in the body first as a bodily or physical sensation. The biological rush of chemicals that gets triggered by the brain as an emotional response is a wave that lasts about 60-90 seconds. That's all. Emotions are temporary. Observing the sensations your body has as the expression of the feeling enables you to come out of your head and to view the emotion more objectively. This can help you to feel safer to allow the emotion to be fully expressed. You can imagine riding the emotional wave knowing that you are safe, and that it is short, and that it will flow out completely if you allow it to. This wave of feeling often starts low and then increases to a peak when you bring your awareness to it and then gradually fades back down.

Allow the emotion to rise in your body as fully as you feel safe to. View the sensations you feel in your body with curiosity and acceptance. There is no judgement in this process. Let go of any concept that what you feel is right or wrong, or good or bad, or that you should or shouldn't be feeling something. Whatever you feel is acceptable. You are acceptable, as you are. All of your feelings are valid. They are valid for YOU, regardless of any comparison to what anyone else is feeling, or whether anyone else has experienced anything worse or better than you. You may find it helpful to scan your body from your feet up to the crown of your head noticing any sensations.

Part 3. Love Yourself for What You Are Feeling

Use the statement starter below to love yourself for whatever you are feeling. This can be an emotion or the physical sensations you are experiencing. Try and be as specific and descriptive as possible. Remember that feelings are temporary sensations and not parts of us, although their energy may be held in our body by a wounded or inner child part of us. An emotion is something you feel not something you are, and it can be helpful to use language to reinforce that, for example saying "I feel sad" rather than "I am sad." Once you start with naming, accepting and loving yourself for one sensation, you may notice another come up. You can keep repeating the process until you feel a sense of completion or peace.

It is good to be aware that emotions often occur in layers. There is an emotion on the surface which is often visibly manifested, and then there is often other emotions underneath that which may not feel as safe to acknowledge or express. Anger is a good example of this. Usually, underlying anger and defensiveness there is fear or a feeling of threat to your sense of safety, and under that fear there is often hurt, pain or grief. When you use this process to release a surface emotion, that may allow underlying emotions to be sensed and felt. All you need to do is notice them and allow the energy of them to flow. You do not need to understand where they come from, or what they mean, or what impact they have had. Sometimes you will receive some clarity or understanding about those things from this practice, but that is not the intention. The intention is simply to feel the movement of the emotional energy as sensations in your body, be in acceptance of it, and allow it to express.

Usually, underlying fear is hurt, pain or lack of safety.
Fear is often expressed as anger or defensiveness.

At the root of it all is something that needs loving or more love.
Love is the antidote of fear.

Statement starter: "I love myself for feeling . . . "

Examples of using the statement starter:

"I love myself for feeling anxious that I won't get this project finished in time"

"I love myself for feeling this tightness in my shoulders"

"I love myself for feeling relaxed right now"

"I love myself for feeling frustrated that I can't quiet my mind at the moment"

"I love myself for feeling unlovable for thinking such dark thoughts about my father when he criticised me"

Do It Now Action Point (a Power of 5 Practice)

Set aside five minutes of quiet time once a day to engage with the three-part Trigger Body Love Practice: identify the trigger experience, feel the sensations in your body, and then love yourself for whatever you are feeling

Remember, you can link this to the practice of Sustaining Pleasure. You could also do this as a meditation practice.

Extra Help

If you have lived in your head most of your life, or have a habit of avoiding or supressing your feelings then you may find it challenging to feel anything at first. Alternatively, you may feel very resistant and fearful that if you open up to your feelings, they will be too strong or too painful to cope with. If this is the case, love yourself for wherever you are at. For example:

"I love myself for feeling afraid to feel"
"I love myself for not feeling anything"
"I love myself for feeling frustrated with this practice"

Offer yourself acceptance for whatever you are feeling. Acceptance creates space for transformation.

Turbo-Boost

Read *Learning to Love Yourself* by Gay Hendricks

Accept Your Feelings Practice Steps

Set aside five minutes of quiet time once a day to engage with the Trigger Body Love Practice.

Turbo boost this practice by reading *Learning to Love* Yourself by Gay Hendricks

Step 7: Choose Your Beliefs

Truth, like beauty, is in the eye of the beholder.

What is a Belief?

A belief is simply a thought that has been consistently repeated. We usually feel like our beliefs need to be, or are, true in some objective way. We desire this in order to feel safe and secure. This is also the reason why we seek validation of our beliefs from others, and why most people adopt the dominant beliefs of the people they are connected with.

However, truth is largely what you choose to focus on and believe, because what you believe your brain will find evidence for. We have an area in our brain called the Reticular Activating System (RAS) which is responsible for filtering all of the sensory information that our body receives and only forwarding the information to your conscious brain that is most important for it to pay attention to. There are certain types of information that are hard-wired to be forwarded such as the sound of your name being called, or anything that threatens your safety or that of your loved ones. Over and above this the filtering system of your RAS is set according to your current interests, and your beliefs. For example, if you develop a belief that people cannot be trusted then your reticular activating system will send through evidence that this is true and filter out examples of how it is not true.

Where Do Our Beliefs Come From?

Most of our beliefs are embedded in early childhood. Human beings have a conscious creative mind, and a subconscious program mind. Our rational conscious mind does not become fully functional until around age seven. Up until then, our mind mainly operates in theta mode, which is the state of imagination and hypnosis. This enables children to quickly and easily download all the information they need to function and survive. They download rules of behaviour by observing the people and the world around them.

This means that in the first seven years of our life we are generally hypnotically programmed with the beliefs of the people we frequently interact with. We are also very ego-centric when we are young, and perceive that people in our environment are the way they are because of us. This means that when the people around us are happy, we conclude in our hard-wired autonomic nervous system that it is because of what we did. The same thing happens when people are sad or angry; we link it to our behaviour.

Vishen Lakhiani, founder and CEO of Mindvalley, has described this as our meaning making machine. Your meaning making machine tries to assign meaning to everything that happens in your life. For example, if your mother sends you to a corner to try to help you learn a behaviour, then you as a child may not understand her intention and your meaning making machine might say, "mum sent me to a corner because there is something wrong with me and she doesn't love me". When a father asks his child to be quiet, then the child's ego-centric meaning making machine might assign this with the meaning "my father doesn't want to hear what I have to say, because what I say isn't important." We assign these meanings to the events in our lives with our limited understanding as children, but when they are repeated or connected to a strong emotional charge, they become embedded in our neural networks and turn into beliefs that we carry with us into adulthood.

You Can Choose Your Beliefs

Most people do not realise they can choose their beliefs. They either live their life almost completely on auto-pilot never really examining what they think and largely avoiding what they feel, or they think they have to believe what everyone else believes because it must be true if everyone believes it, and we have a very strong need to be included as part of a secure social group. However, you can choose your beliefs. You are the creator of your life and you have the power and permission to choose thoughts that serve you and thoughts that make you feel good. Most of what we believe is simply social conditioning. You can begin to question what you believe. Not questioning in terms of where did your beliefs come from, which can lead to blame and focusing on what you don't want. You don't really need to know where your beliefs came from, only what they currently are.

When you become conscious of a belief that you want to examine or question, three beneficial questions to ask are:

- ➢ Does this belief serve me?
- ➢ Does this thought make me feel good?
- ➢ Do I want to continue to believe this?

How to Deactivate Limiting Beliefs

Many people talk about letting go of limiting beliefs. The concept of letting go can be quite challenging. I prefer to think in terms of deactivating limiting beliefs. Rather than trying to not think them (let them go), it is easier to reduce their influence; their power and control.

I do not think that you need to understand why you developed the beliefs you have. It is human nature to want to try and understand, but going back into past memories, and talking and thinking about past experiences often turns your focus to things that are painful. Remember, where focus goes, energy flows, and you don't want to give energy to what you don't want, you want to give energy to creating something new moving forward. You do not need to know how you developed a certain belief in order to deactivate it. You do not need to bring up and rehash old experiences and hurts and understand why you think and feel the way you do. Simply start from where you are at now. Accept that for whatever reason you currently have a certain pattern of thinking or belief. Changing your beliefs is an ongoing process. It involves consistently increasing your awareness of what you are thinking, and choosing to think positive thoughts which are in line with the life you want to create and the person you want to be.

From this place of conscious knowing, an awakening happens. You are now more present in the moment, allowing you to make a new choice. When you can choose, you are now in freedom.
Jennifer McLean - Author and speaker
on transformation and healing

Be compassionate with yourself. This is the same as learning any new skill. It takes consistent practice, and sometimes you will be in flow and sometimes you won't. When you find yourself thinking negative thoughts, or become aware of a limiting belief you have, don't fight it or despair over it because what we resist, persists. See it as an experience of awareness and learning. You can use empowering statements such as:

> "This is what I used to think, but I can now choose another thought which serves me better", or,

> "I am thankful that I am becoming more conscious of what I think because awareness is the first step to growing."

You can also use the Trigger Body Love process to help bring acceptance, space and release to limiting beliefs. For example:

> "I love myself for believing that I don't have enough time to do what I want to do"

> "I love myself for feeling frustrated that I was thinking negative thoughts about myself this afternoon."

Remember to link your feelings to specific situations as much as possible, rather than generalising. For example, "I love myself for feeling hopeless that I can't control my thoughts at the moment." Rather than "I love myself for feeling hopeless that I can never control my thoughts." It is easier for us to accept one instance of a behaviour and see that we can choose to do something differently going forward, as opposed to seeing it as something we always do (and it is usually not true that we always do it). It is about seeing it as a behaviour rather than an identity; I was doing that rather than I am that.

3 Part Belief Deactivation Process: Recognise, Decide, Focus

RECOGNISE your current beliefs

DECIDE what you want to believe
FOCUS on what you want

Recognise Your Current Beliefs

The first step in deactivating beliefs that no longer serve you is to become aware of what you believe currently. Here are some practices you can try to become more aware of what you are repeatedly thinking:

What do you repeatedly complain about?

This can be obvious, for example a single woman who often complains that there are no good men available clearly has that belief going on. For a person who frequently talks about people treating them disrespectfully, the surface belief attached to that is people don't respect me, and there is probably also underlying root beliefs such as "I am not worthy of respect", or "people are not interested in what I say." The Trigger Body Love process may help you become conscious of deeper core beliefs. For extra support you could have sessions with a quality life coach who is trained in embodiment modalities.

Listen to what you say in conversation

What you complain about reveals what you feel resistant to and limited by. What you repeatedly say indicates your beliefs about yourself and life. Deeper subconscious beliefs are more likely to show up in what you say when you are relaxed and speaking unguardedly. This is why conversations with strangers, or people you have no emotional investment with, can often lead to you experiencing greater clarity or insight through the conversation.

Notice when you say "I can't"

This is similar to noticing what you complain about. When you say I can't do something or have something, then the reason why is probably a limiting belief. For example, if you think, "I can't be honest about my feelings with my partner because they might get angry", then it likely stems from beliefs such as "I need to do whatever it takes to keep peace in my relationships", or "anger is unsafe".

Journaling

There are many different ways to journal. You can use reflective questions to guide you, or create a visual journal with drawings and words, or engage in stream of consciousness journaling where you just put pen to paper and write whatever comes to mind in that moment or around a given topic.

Listen to what you say to your children

What are some common statements you make to your children if you have children? It is also interesting to notice when you sound like your parents. What you say signals beliefs you hold and if you say the same things your parents said it points to subconscious programming you have from them. What are your parental mantras? They might be statements like: "you can't have everything you want", "money doesn't grow on trees", "life isn't fair" etc.

Identify what you consistently lack

About 95% of your life is created by your subconscious programs. Therefore, your life is a print-out of these programs. The things that come into your life easily and abundantly do so because you have subconscious programs that say it is comfortable to accept those. Anything that you work hard at, or struggle over, or put a lot of effort into making manifest are things that your subconscious programming does not support you having. This is usually because your subconscious views it as unfamiliar and therefore unsafe, or because you have a belief that you are not worthy or deserving of it.

The amount of money you have is usually a classic example of this. Most of us want more money, but if money is not flowing freely to you, it is because your nervous system doesn't feel safe to have more money and/or you have limiting beliefs around it such as: "money is the root of all evil and therefore bad/sinful", "I don't have enough money", "there is not enough money", "money is hard to get", or "more money means more problems".

Think of a problem or situation in your life that you are struggling with or where you feel stuck, and write a story about it as if it were happening to someone else. Think of why the character in the story might be having this issue, or why they feel like they can't do certain options. What beliefs might this character be under the influence of? Doing this helps us to see the problem from a broader perspective, and reduces the emotional charge and stress which frees up our creative thinking.

Decide What You Want to Believe

There is power in decision so decide what you want to believe. When you make a clear decision about what you want and commit to moving towards it then momentum starts to happen. You may encounter a little resistance in the beginning as the flow of energy shifts, but eventually, if you keep moving forward towards the outcome you want, then energy will begin to flow with you.

I think of it like the whirlpools we used to make in swimming pools as children. We would all start walking around the outside of the pool in the same direction. At first it would be hard because the water was static and we were trying to get it moving, but eventually the water would begin to shift and flow with us and after a while the energy of the water flowing in the direction we were going was so strong that we could stop making any effort and the force of the water would carry us. Then, we would all make the decision to try going against the flow of the water. This was really hard because so much momentum had built up flowing in the opposite direction, but as we persisted, we would be able to reverse the energy of the water and get it flowing strongly the other way. The movement of energy in life works in the same way, and in the same way you are the decider. You are the force that directs the flow.

Focus on What You Want

Consistently choose to focus, and refocus, on the thoughts you want to think and the beliefs that you want to hold. This is a moment-by-moment choice and practice. You get better at it, but it is something that you will always have to do like choosing what to eat. You need to consistently choose to nourish your body, and in the same way you need to consistently choose to nourish your mind.

Here are 4 things you can do to focus your mind in nourishing ways:

Be present
When you are present, you are conscious of what you are thinking, and choosing to think and focus on, which takes you out of your old subconscious programs.

Sustain pleasure
When you experience any positive emotion try and stay in it and increase it as much as possible. (see Step 5 for more details on practicing being present and sustaining pleasure).

Get Curious
Use curious mind opening statement starters to overcome resistance and activate your creative imagination. For example:

> What if I could believe that [desired belief]
> What would it take for me to believe that [desired belief]
> How can I gather evidence to support the belief that . . .

Look for evidence that what you want is possible
When you begin to look for evidence of the positive things you want to see, you'll begin to notice more and more examples of them. This is because you have shifted your focus and adopted a new dominant thought. Our RAS, and quantum physics determine that we attract what we think about; our thoughts become things.

You will always find what you are looking for

When someone receives something that you want, celebrate with them because it means it is possible for you to receive that too. When someone achieves something you want to achieve, celebrate, because it means it is possible for you to do that too. Let go of not knowing how this could happen for you, and just know with gratitude that what you want is possible in the universe.

Thank you, more please

Do It Now Action Point

We have talked about quite a lot of things in this Step, and you may not be able to implement it all in one week. Take one practice that is most relevant to where you are at and focus on that for the next week, and remember that once again there are overlaps and some of the practices for this step are also incorporated into other steps.

If the concept of choosing your beliefs is very new to you, then you can just focus on one practice which will help you to become more aware of your beliefs and make the unconscious, conscious such as journaling for five minutes every day.

If you are fairly aware of what your common patterns of thought are then you may want to focus more on deactivating old beliefs and embedding new ones. In this case you can choose to decide on one or two new beliefs that are most important to you at this point in your life to wire into your brain. This practice alone is powerful, the deciding, so you may wish to just do that, or choose to implement one of the practices for focusing on what you want.

Keep it simple and doable for you.
Remember, how do you eat an elephant? One bite at a time.

Extra Help

The language that we use can have a significant effect on how we perceive ourselves and the world around us. Below are some empowering rephrases which you can use to help shift limiting beliefs. When you say something using the words on the left, you can rephrase your statement using the phrase on the right.

I can't   >   *How can I*

I should   >   *I could*

I've got to   >   *I get to*

I don't like   >   *I like*

It's probably not
going to happen   > *It's possible for it to happen*

Why is this
happening to me?   > *How is this happening for me?*

Turbo-Boost

Bin It and Pin It Game (Power of 5 Practice)

Studies have shown that writing our thoughts down on a piece of paper and then throwing it away helps us to discharge those thoughts. The opposite has also been shown to occur, that when we write a thought down on a piece of paper and carry it around then we are likely to become attached to it. The *Bin It and Pin It* game uses this concept to help you deactivate negative and limiting beliefs, and embed new positive, empowering ones. You can do this as a Power of 5 exercise and set a timer for two minutes to write down all the negative, limiting thoughts you have on a subject and then throw the pieces of paper in a rubbish bin. Then, set the timer for two minutes again and write out the beliefs about the subject you want to embed and put them somewhere you can become attached to them. This may be pinning them to a wall or bathroom mirror, or writing them on a piece of paper to put in your handbag, or slip under a clear phone case, or tuck into your wallet.

This practice can also be done on the go. Every time you become aware that you are thinking a negative thought, write it down on a piece of paper and throw it in the bin, then write out a positive thought you want to believe instead and "pin it" somewhere. You can also do this process as a visualisation if pen and paper are not readily available. Imagine writing the belief you want to discard on a piece of paper and throwing it in the rubbish, and then imagine writing the positive belief you want to attach/embed on a piece of paper and pinning it in front of you.

Choose Your Beliefs Practice Steps

> ➢ Pick one practice to focus on this week that fits with where you are at in terms of choosing your beliefs: recognising, deciding or focusing.

➢ Use language re-phrases and curiosity statement starters to open your mind to new beliefs which serve you.

➢ Turbo Boost deactivating negative, limiting beliefs and embedding new positive, empowering ones by playing the Bin It and Pin It game.

Step 8: Know Your Inherent Worth

The Biggest Lie We Believe

One of the most common limiting beliefs is "I am not enough". This belief stems partly from criticisms we receive, and imbibed societal beliefs about the deficiency of human beings, and partly from our ego-centric nature as children. Remember from Step 7 that as young children, we believe that people in our environment are the way they are because of us. When the people around us are happy, we believe in our hard-wired autonomic nervous system that they feel this way because of what we did. The same thing happens when people are sad or angry; we link it to our behaviour. This leads us to create a belief in our own deficiency, but it is the way we make sense of our environment. As a child, when you feel uncomfortable and you don't know why, then the only way your brain can make sense of it in your ego-centric state is to believe that there is something wrong with you.

As ego-centric children we can also believe that if there is something wrong with our parents then we can fix it by being better. Our subconscious meaning maker may conclude that "If I am a better person then my parents will stop fighting", or "If I work harder at being tidy then mum won't feel so sad", or "If I do better in school my dad will want to spend more time with me". Children frequently conclude that when something is wrong, it must be because of them. For example, a child may reason: "It must be my fault if my parent is mean to me, or can't love me. I must be unlovable."

The Pressure to be a Better Person

Children can start to carry the emotional baggage of the family and take on the burden: "If only I could do more." This pressure to be a better person can continue into adulthood. I also see the call to be a better person promoted a lot in personal development material. I believe that as eternal energy in physical form (a soul in a body) that we are wired to desire expansion. However, I believe this expansion is in terms of greater alignment with our true selves, and experience of physical reality. The word "better" has moral judgement attached to it, and to say that you need to be better indicates that you are not already enough. A belief that you need to be better in some way stems from the belief: "I am not enough".

Unworthiness, Overwork and Procrastination

A belief that you are unworthy often underlies two common patterns of behaviour: overworking and procrastinating. When people consistently overwork, over-give and/or overproduce they are usually subconsciously, or sometimes consciously, feeling a need to prove themselves or earn love and respect. The root of that is a low sense of your own worthiness. Unworthiness can also be expressed as the opposite of this as procrastination or avoiding taking action. This is normally due to fear of failure. These are actually typical threat responses: fight, flight and freeze. Overworking is fight, and procrastination and avoidance is flight or freeze. When you feel unworthy you also feel unsafe, and when you feel unsafe, your body's stress and survival system kicks in. To begin to unravel this, you need to first calm and regulate your nervous system and soothe it out of sympathetic stress mode using all the types of practices listed in Step 3 which release feel good chemicals in your body, and then rewire your beliefs about your worthiness.

Unworthiness and Failure

Many people connect failure to their worthiness. It is common in most societies to celebrate the winners and denigrate the losers. Failure is frequently associated with embarrassment, humiliation and shame. However, everybody fails from time to time. When you fail it does not mean that you are a failure, or that you are useless, or that you are not good enough. It just means that you did something that didn't work out in the way expected or the way you wanted this time. Most highly successful people are highly successful because they have learned to fail successfully. You fail successfully by choosing not to see failure as determining your worth, but as information gathering and learning. You also fail successfully by staying focused on what you are wanting to experience and achieve rather than the way others are judging you from their external viewpoint. I was married and divorced twice and then dated a lot in my later forties. While I was having my dating experiences I was writing about relationships and I had more than one person say to me that I didn't have a valid basis to write about relationships because I had not had a successful one. That was their view and judgement. My intention was to learn how to create a great relationship and for me, one way to learn how to do that was to have lots of contrasting experiences to receive different information from. The definition of what constitutes success and failure is also subjective. For example, many people determine that a relationship is successful if it lasts a long time, whereas I define a successful relationship as one which uplifts or expands the people involved no matter what length of time that occurs over.

You are Inherently Worthy

Worthiness is often seen to be conditional. For example, it was and still is a commonly held belief that women need to be good and pure to be worthy of love. I would argue though, that you are inherently worthy as a created living being. We recognise that worth in new-born babies, but then quite quickly our worth becomes linked to our behaviour, both in the eyes of other people and ourselves. Our inherent worth never changes, only our perception of it does. You may be familiar with the banknote analogy of self-worth. Let's say I offer you a current $100 note. You would recognise its value and want to have it. What if I told you it was an older note that had been in circulation for a while and was wrinkly and faded? Its inherent value of $100 would still be the same, even if it was well-used. What if I stood on it and scrunched it into the mud? It would still be worth $100. What if I told you that this $100 note had been used to buy drugs? You would still recognise that it is worth $100 no matter how it had been used in the past. You are the same. No matter what your age, even if you've been beaten up and marked by life, even if you have been involved in illegal, damaging or unhealthy experiences, your inherent worth never changes.

Your sense of value, your importance, who you are is not determined by the opinion, and the approval, of others, but it's determined by yourself. It's determined by the mere fact that you are a living, breathing, amazing, unique, unrepeatable, never been before created human being on this planet and there is no one like you, and you are extraordinary, and it's you owning that.
\- Matthew Boggs

There is a tendency to see it as humility to down-play our abilities and achievements, but the root of this belief is fear. Fear that we are not enough. Fear that we are wrong, or will make a mistake and be judged by others. Fear of rejection and criticism if we shine bright and stand out. However, when we choose not to shine the full light of who we are, then we deny other people the opportunity to receive from that.

If you choose not to shine,
you rob others of your light.

You are a unique creation with a unique contribution to offer the world. Moreover, when we give ourselves permission to own our greatness, by our example we give other people permission to do so too. What if everyone could be great? What if there was no limit to how great we could all be?

We aren't here to prove our worth or worthiness. . .
Our existence itself is proof of our worth, since nothing blinks from
un-manifest into manifest without a reason and purpose.
You are enough. Exactly as you are.
I believe you are not simply here to DO something great . . .
I believe you ARE something great, exactly as you are
Jesse Elder – Speaker, Writer, Philosopher

Abraham Hicks offers a very simple barometer for recognising your inherent worth; that you can know whether a thought is in line with your higher inner being or not by how it makes you feel. If a thought feels light, loving, and expansive then it is in line with what your inner being (soul) knows to be true. If it feels uncomfortable, restricting, sad, guilty or fearful then it is not. In other words, if a thought makes you feel good it is aligned with your inner truth, and if it doesn't then it is not. When you think thoughts like "I am lovable" and "I am powerful" they feel light and good. Thinking thoughts like "I hate myself" and "I am unsupported" feel heavy and contracting.

Your body also demonstrates why you are wired to recognise your self-worth. Kinesiology practices show that when you think positive thoughts about yourself such as "I am strong", "people like me", and "I am capable" then you have robust muscle strength. When you think negative thoughts such as "I am weak", "I can't get it right", and "I'm an idiot" then your muscle strength decreases. One of the reasons for this is that they put your body into a stress response. Negative thoughts affect your nervous system. Research has shown that high levels of negative thinking can cause brain degeneration, cardiovascular problems, lowered immunity and digestive issues.

How to Feel Greater Self-Worth

The issue is not that you are not enough, and not worthy. The issue is that you do not *perceive* yourself as enough and as worthy. The issue is one of belief. To feel greater self-worth, you need to rewire your brain by creating habits of positive thought about yourself.

What you present to your mind it will present right back to you. . .
Your mind believes everything you tell it. . . Your mind doesn't
care if what you tell it is right or wrong, good or bad,
healthy or unhealthy, it just lets it in . . .
why not tell it amazing things? You can make anything true
so you might as well make amazing things true
- Marisa Peer

Below are six practices you can use to rewire your brain to develop greater self-worth:

Nod Your Head (Power of 5 Practice)
There is a strong connection between our body and mind. Both your thoughts and your body will perform at their highest levels when your nervous system is functioning optimally. One of the most important areas for optimal functioning of the nervous system is where your spinal cord meets your brain. This area is protected by your first cervical vertebrae called the Atlas. When the nervous system is compromised due to the Atlas vertebrae being out of place it distorts normal brain to body, and body to brain, signals. This spinal issue can cause painful past memories stored in your hippocampus, and also your current daily issues, which are new memories in your pre-frontal lobe, to replay over and over in your thoughts. A number of psychological and emotional issues can result from this including thoughts that we are not good enough.

A simple practice that you can do at home to correct spinal alignment, and stimulate blood and energy flow from the brain through the spinal cord is to nod your head as if you were nodding in agreement with something Try standing with your shoulders relaxed and down and direct your mental focus to the place at the lower tips of your shoulder blades behind your heart centre. This is the root of your neck. A neutral head is anchored deep in the upper back through this neck root, and all of its movements are initiated from and flow out of this source. Now nod your head up and down slowly and consciously by pushing up and drawing down from the neck root. Aim to do 20-30 repetitions each day. You can incorporate your breathing into this practice too and explore breathing out as you push up from your neck root and lower your head and in as you draw your head back up, and then reverse the breath pattern. Notice how each way of breathing feels in your body. If you have significant issues with negative thoughts or depression, then it may be beneficial to see a quality chiropractor to correct your spinal alignment.

Affirm You Are Enough (Power of 5 Practice)

While I am not generally a proponent of affirmations because they can promote emotional and energetic resistance if we do not believe them, as Rapid Transformational Therapy trainer and best-selling author Marisa Peer teaches, our soul agrees with the statement "I am enough". In Abraham Hicks terms, it is in line with what your higher self knows to be true. If you say something like "I am a millionaire" when you are not, your conscious brain knows it is not true, but it is also not a Universal truth of your inner soul, therefore it can create resistance because you want it, but you don't have it. Statements like "I am enough", "I am strong", and "I am worthy" may not agree with your subconscious programming, but they align with your soul truth and therefore create no energetic resistance. Marisa Peer advocates repeating an "I am enough" affirmation on a daily basis. She has some creative ideas about how to add it to your subconscious data files:

> Say it to yourself in the mirror each day
> Write it on mirrors around the house
> Make it your password
> Write it daily (you could write it at the start of your daily gratitude or journaling practice)

Give Your Negative Voice a Separate Identity

Recognise that the self-critical voice in your head is not your own. Remember that you are inherently worthy. Remember that thoughts that align with your higher self, feel good. If the voice in your head is saying something mean or critical about you then it is not your own true voice. It is a voice that has been downloaded, manipulated and installed in you. It is the voice of other people's beliefs that you have taken on for yourself. The next time you become aware that you are internally, or verbally, beating yourself up, ask yourself: "Who is really saying this? Whose voice is this?"

This is not about blame; it is about awareness. It may help to play creatively with this and give your negative inner voice a made-up identity and name that helps you to disassociate yourself from those thoughts. When we step back and become an observer of our thoughts it reduces the emotional charge of them. It is the emotional charge connected with thoughts that gives them real strength.

Become Aware of Dramatic Exaggerations

Your brain responds the same way whether a stimulus comes through your physical senses, is imagined or is verbalised. The words you say have impact, not just for others, but for you. It is quite common for people to use exaggerated language like "I'll die if he leaves me", "my job is killing me", and "I'm starving". This might make for more interesting conversation, but it also programmes your brain.

Exaggerated negative statements like this indicate to your brain that you are threatened and unsafe. As a result, your brain puts your body in survival, fight or flight (stress) mode. Statements like this also dis-empower you. When you say something like "my job is killing me" the underlying message your brain receives is "I am not coping", "I am over-whelmed", "I am not in control of this situation", and "I feel unsafe". All this feeds the belief, "I am not enough". Speaking this way is common practice in modern Westernised society. When you say something positive it can feel a little strange and uncomfortable. However, this is simply habit and common practice that you can work to change. Awareness is the first step, then focus on being more conscious with what you are saying to program your brain with what you want to be thinking. If you make an exaggerated negative statement and then become aware of what you've said, recognise that it isn't actually true (you could also assign it to your created other identity as per Give Your Negative Voice a Separate Identity above), and say something positive and/or solution based to balance it out. As you continue to focus it will become more natural to speak using positive, empowered language.

Give Your Mind Clear, Proactive Instructions

When we fail at something it can reinforce thoughts that we are not enough. Failure can often occur due to faulty brain programming. Remember, "Your mind believes everything you tell it. . . Your mind doesn't care if what you tell it is right or wrong, good or bad, healthy or unhealthy, it just lets it in" (Marissa Peer). Therefore, be very conscious about the instructions you give your brain through the thoughts you think.

If you would like to lose weight, for example, but you keep thinking that it is such a chore to eat healthy food, and that all healthy food tastes horrible, and you'll die if you eat another veggie stick, and you love eating cake, and it's much better to eat pizza, and you'd rather have a chocolate bar on the way home than wait to eat a healthy dinner, then you are programming your brain to see healthy food as an undesirable threat and programming in the unhealthy habit you want to change. Give your brain clear specific instructions by consciously thinking thoughts about what you choose to desire. Be aware that you may not desire this fully yet, but it is something you want to want.

This also links in to the positive rephrase statements included in Step 7. For example: instead of thinking/saying: "I need to go to the gym" or "I have to go to the gym" think "I get to go to the gym", or "I could go to the gym", or "I want to go to the gym". Using the words "have to", "need to" or "should" indicates that you are responding to external pressure. This will feel like you are forcing yourself, and having to use willpower to complete the stated action. These statements have a low vibration and feel heavy and hard. Consequently, there is a high likelihood that you will resist or avoid the action. Using the words "get to", "could", or "want to" indicate you are choosing this action for yourself. They suggest this is something you desire. These statements have a high vibration and feel light, exciting and decisive. Consequently, there is a high likelihood that you will take action and experience success.

Give Yourself a Fresh Start Every-day

I am new in this new day

When you wake up each day, think of yourself as being new into this new day; a daily fresh start. The past only exists in our mind, and only has power if we give it power. It may help to visualise walking through a door away from all that is in your past, closing the door behind you, then turning and walking forward into the new day.

There is no such thing as the past, nor the future.
These are mere words used to describe an imaginary event
that can only be created in the present.
- Jesse Elder

Develop a growth mind-set where you accept that learning anything involves improvement with practice, and that not getting it right and making mistakes are simply part of the process of growth. Be compassionate with yourself as you grow. Focus on "I am getting better at this" rather than "I must master this".

How to Manage Destructive Criticism

The best way to manage criticism from other people is to look to yourself for your self-worth, not others. When you look to others for validation and approval then you have no control over the conditions you are basing your beliefs on. You cannot truly control others, and you cannot know everything that motivates them to do what they do. When you make your self-worth dependent on what others say and do in regards to you, you tend to remain in a child-like state of ego-centricity where you interpret other people's actions in terms of yourself. For example, you may think that the guy you like didn't phone you because he doesn't like you, when in actual fact there could have been all sorts of reasons why he didn't, most of which are not to do with you.

Standing in your power to choose your own beliefs about your self-worth enables you to let go of taking everything personally. Feeling secure in yourself releases you from needing the attention of others. As you take responsibility for your own feelings, needs and beliefs, you detach yourself from the opinion of others and become empowered to choose not to take on destructive criticism. Criticism from others only affects you if you let it in. You always have a choice to not accept destructive criticism.

Do It Now Action Point

Choose one of the practices to help you develop greater self-worth and incorporate it into your daily routine this week.

> ➢ Nod Your Head

> ➢ Affirm You are Enough

> ➢ Give Your Negative Voice a Separate Identity

> ➢ Be Aware of Dramatic Exaggerations

> ➢ Give Your Mind Clear, Proactive Instructions

> ➢ Give Yourself a Fresh Start Every Day

Extra Help

Be compassionate with yourself. Changing your beliefs and habitual patterns of thought and behaviour is a moment by moment, day by day choice and growth process. The most important thing is to keep taking steps forward no matter how small they are. Give yourself time. If you are stuck with even wanting to want positive things in your life, or have a powerful belief that change isn't possible, which is often rooted in the belief "I am not enough" and/or "I deserve to be punished/unhappy", then you can try starting with the statement "I want to want to . . ."

For example:

"I want to want to believe that I am allowed to feel happy"

"I want to want to forgive myself"

"I want to want to believe that I can be successful"

"I want to want to go for a walk each day"

Turbo-Boost

Do more than one of the practices for rewiring your brain to develop greater self-worth. You can combine some of the practices. For example, nod your head while you say the affirmation "I am enough". You could do this as a daily meditation practice. Or, start the day with the combination affirmation: "I am enough. I am new into this new day."

Know Your Inherent Worth Practice Steps

> ➤ Choose one of the practices to help you develop greater self-worth and incorporate it into your daily routine this week.

> ➤ Be compassionate with yourself, and if you feel as though you are struggling to change your beliefs and rewire your brain, then try using the statement "I want to want to . . . "

> ➤ Turbo Boost rewiring your brain by doing more than one of the practices each day, and by combining practices where possible.

Step 9: Fill Your Own Love Bucket

Most people look to other people to get love and to make themselves feel loved. The problem with this is that it is conditional upon the actions of other people and we cannot control the actions of others. This means that our sense of being loved or unloved rises and falls as we interpret what other people do in relation to us, and it can lead to us trying various ways to control and manipulate the people we seek love from.

There is a common belief that loving and appreciating yourself is narcissistic and self-absorbed. Actually, the opposite is true. People who are narcissistic and self-absorbed are internally very insecure and also prone to self-loathing. This is why they usually take from others, because they have big holes to fill in their emotional needs. People with narcissistic personality disorder require constant, excessive admiration because they have secret feelings of insecurity and shame. We are more selfish when we do not love ourselves because we look to others to give us the love we need. When we do not fill our own love tank, we often give love to get love in return. We give from a place of need. Connecting with your true self and becoming your own source of fulfilment, allows you to give out of overflow and naturally become a giver. When you give love to yourself you can also give it freely to others. You become secure as your own source of fulfilment, and so feel no need to take from others. In doing so you also release others from having to make you happy – something that is impossible for them to do.

How to Fill Your Own Love Bucket

Here are some simple, fast, effective practices you can use in your daily life to fill up your own love bucket.

Choose to Love Yourself as You Are (Power of 5)
Every time you look at yourself in the mirror you can say to yourself: "I choose to love you as you are". Adding "I choose" at the start of the affirmation helps your brain to receive it, even if you do not currently believe that you love yourself as you are. If you like you can combine this with the affirmation "I am enough"; "I choose to love myself as I am and I am enough."

Appreciate What You Have Achieved (Power of 5)
Another simple practice you can do is to take a few minutes to write or think about what you have achieved today, and to feel appreciation and pride for that. I included this in Step 1 of this book as part of the daily gratitude practice. You can expand this into an achievement board or wall. This is a specific place in your home or office where you display mementoes and evidence of positive things you have achieved. If you set up an achievement board or wall aim to take time to reflect on it daily and add to it regularly. Remember, achievements can be having a special moment of connection with your children, or helping someone, or making time to do something you enjoy as well as gaining an external qualification or acknowledgement, or achieving a goal.

Appreciate Who You Are (Power of 5 practice)
Again, this has been included as part of the daily gratitude practice in Step 1. Here are some suggestions of what you can appreciate yourself for:

- skills and talents you have

- kindnesses you showed

- ways in which you honoured yourself

- how you are becoming more aware of what your thoughts are

- how you've started moving your body for pleasure

- how you're getting better at focusing on the positive things you want

Date Yourself

From time to time imagine you are on a date with yourself. Speak to yourself as a lover would speak to you. Make love to yourself - I do not mean make love in the sexual sense here (although connecting with your own sexual energy can also be very healing and empowering). I mean it in the traditional sense of courting or wooing as in being loving and attentive. Have fun with this practice.

> You could sing love songs to yourself.
> You could buy yourself flowers.
> You could give yourself a massage.

If it is good for us to express love to others in this way, then logically it must also be good to express love to ourselves in this way. You are just as worthy of love as anyone else. The only reason it feels strange is because of the beliefs we have been taught about it.

Ask This Key Question When Making Decisions

When it comes to making decisions, most of us want to know how to make the right one. Usually, we think about something being right in ethical or religious terms. However, this is often in conflict with what we want, or know in our heart. This creates the age-old head versus heart dilemma, and the question of which one should you listen to. Traditionally, thinking with the head is seen as the better option. This is possibly because it is a masculine trait, and most human societies have always been patriarchal. However, often following our head does not make us feel happy. We might feel proud that we have done the right thing, or that we have followed a rational plan of action. Yet if that decision was not in line with what we truly wanted, then we may also feel conflicted, frustrated, resentful and/or sad. If this is the case, then we have not honoured ourselves in our decision, and our love bucket will be emptied rather than filled.

One way to make a decision that fills our love bucket is to base it on this key question:

What would I do if I truly loved myself?

Asking this question usually cuts through all the whirling possible options based around could, should and what other people want, and reveals the clear option that respects you, and what you truly want. At times making decisions based on doing what is truly loving to yourself means disappointing others. Some people find this challenging. Ultimately though, you are the only person you are responsible for, and responsible to. Also, when you do not honour your own needs, you also dishonour others because you are not being truthful. There is dishonesty if you say one thing, but secretly want something else. This creates dis-ease within you, and also withholding in your relationships with others.

Stop Settling (Power of 5 practice)

Regularly take time to reflect on the question: "how am I settling for less than I deserve?" You could make it a daily five-minute meditation or journaling prompt for this week.

Stop settling for internal criticism and put-downs. Choose not to accept them.

Stop settling for last place. Do you always sacrifice your needs/wants and put yourself last? Over-giving does not lead to others giving back to you - it leads to neglect. You are allowed to ask for your needs to be met. Treat yourself, and others, fairly.

Stop settling for living in fear.

Stop settling for doing things just because you think you should.

Stop settling for being treated disrespectfully.

Stop settling for your attention being sucked into people and things that don't serve you and take you forward.

Claim your worth.
You are so very valuable

Do It Now Action Point

Choose one of the practices to help you fill your own love tank, and incorporate it into your daily routine this week. Here is a list of the practices to choose from:

> Say the affirmation "I choose to love myself, just as I am" each time you look in a mirror – you could write it on the mirror to remind you.

> Appreciate what you have achieved

> Appreciate who you are

> Date yourself

> Ask "what would I do if I truly loved myself" when making decisions

> Reflect on the question: "How am I settling for less than I deserve?"

Extra Help

If you find it very difficult to think of things you appreciate about yourself, or to make decisions that honour your needs rather than doing what pleases others, then, as we talked about in Step 8, you can start with repeating affirmations that have statement starters which help you begin to make gentle shifts to want to want to love yourself. For example:

> "I want to want to believe that I am allowed to love myself"

> "I want to want to choose to love myself as I am"

If you are feeling overwhelmed at the thought of introducing another new practice this week, then simply focus on the Step 1 gratitude practice which also includes the Appreciate What You Have Achieved, and Appreciate Who You Are practices from this step.

Turbo-Boost

Do more than one of the practices for filling your love bucket. You can combine practices. For example, each day you could do five minutes of journaling or meditation reflecting on "How am I settling for less than I deserve?" and finish it by saying the affirmation "I choose to love myself as I am and I am enough." Alternatively, you could take yourself on a date and look back through old photos reflecting on what you have achieved in the past. Remember to encourage and compliment yourself as an ideal lover would.

Fill Your Own Love Bucket Practice Steps

> ➢ Choose one of the practices to help you fill your own love

bucket and incorporate it into your daily routine this week.

➢ Be compassionate with yourself, and if you feel as though you are struggling to believe you are allowed to love yourself, then try using the statement "I want to believe that I am allowed to love myself" or even, "I want to want to believe that I am allowed to love myself".

➢ If you feel like you have too much else going on to incorporate another new practice this week then focus on the Step 1 gratitude practice which also includes the *Appreciate What You Have Achieved*, and *Appreciate Who You Are* practices from this step.

➢ Turbo Boost filling your love bucket by doing more than one of the practices each day, and by combining practices where possible.

Step 10: Create Connection

Connection is one of the top keys to happiness, specifically:
connection to your true self
connection with a supportive group of people
connection to a greater purpose
connection to a higher consciousness

We have already covered a number of aspects of connecting to your true self which involves being tuned in to your thoughts and feelings, and accepting and loving yourself as you are. In this step, I want to focus on the second, third and fourth aspects of connection.

Connect with a Supportive Group of Friends

Our default state is connection. We are social creatures, and have been for eons. . .

Social isolation is the best-established, most robust social or psychological risk factor for disease out there.
Nothing can compete.
- Professor Steven Cole

Belonging to a supportive social network, whether that be of friends or family members or both, is crucial to health and happiness, even for introverts like me. In an article titled *Can a Lack of Love Be Deadly*, Ines Varela-Silva wrote of children in orphanages that "when emotional deprivation and lack of love occur, physical growth slows down or stops. The body enters into a survival mode where vital, basic physiological functions are preserved at the cost of physical, mental, and social development. The longer the child is in survival mode, the more permanent and negative the effects will be." Remember from Step 3: Get Chemical Help, our bodies are wired to release feel good and anti-inflammatory chemicals when we experience affectionate touch with other people. We even have a homone specifically to help us bond with others which is called oxytocin. To function at an optimal level physically, mentally and emotionally we need to connect with other people.

However, it is important to be discerning about who we allow into our energetic space, and who we choose to spend our time with. We have a tendency to become like the people we spend time with. Peer pressure may affect you more strongly when you are younger, but we are still susceptible to it as adults.

I would never tell you to dump your old friends, but I will tell you that loneliness is contagious, unhappiness is contagious, bad health behaviors — they're all measurably contagious. So, one of the best things you can do to stack your deck in favor of happiness is to proactively bring happy people into your network. And not just happy [ones]. It has to be people who care about you."
- Dan Buettner – author of The Blue Zones of Happiness

Cultivate a supportive group of people who will encourage you to be who you want to be and go where you want to go in life. If you try to carry others, you will both be weighed down and struggle to move forward. Focus your time and energy on people who will help you to fly in the updraft they create with their own lives.

Connect to a Greater Purpose

This doesn't mean that, like the Blues Brothers from the movie of the same name, you have to go on a mission from God. It just means we feel happier when we connect to a purpose that is bigger than ourselves. This may mean setting the intention of raising happy, healthy, caring children. It may mean giving your time in volunteer service somehow. It might mean using the profits from your business to support a charitable cause or promote a positive message.

Your passion can also be your greater purpose. Whatever lights you up, when you engage in it and share it, will also uplift others, and that is contributing to a greater purpose. People often equate greater purpose with sacrifice and work, but that does not have to be the case, and I propose that it is more beneficial when you are serving from a place of your own joy. If you are connecting to a higher purpose that feels heavy with work and sacrifice to you, then you are bringing low vibration negative energy to what you are doing, and that is going to mean that the positive impact of your contribution will be limited. Connecting to your greater purpose is about sharing, giving back or giving out in a way that resonates with your true self.

Connect to a Higher Consciousness

By connecting to a higher consciousness, I do not necessarily mean joining a particular religion, or adhering to a certain set of spiritual beliefs, although if that serves you to express this aspect of connection then that is all good. What I mean by connecting to a higher consciousness is having a sense that there is a Universal energy of some sort that flows through all things and gives meaning to our existence. As humans we seek meaning, and we desire that our lives are meaningful in some way.

Humans have a primal sense that there is something in this universe higher than ourselves, as evidenced by the spiritual beliefs of tribal peoples, and the vast number of people who have religious beliefs. We may give different interpretations to that higher consciousness, but most people are aware of it in some way. There is meaning, and purpose and power in connecting with that higher consciousness. Some people connect to it by being in nature, some people through meditation, some people through shamanic practices, some people through music, some people through prayer, and some people sense it when they create art. Find a way that resonates with you. My advice would be to let go of needing your beliefs around this topic to be true in any objective sense. Choose beliefs that speak to your soul, and empower you to expand as a limitless being of love.

Spirituality is recognizing and celebrating that we are all inextricably connected to each other by a power greater than all of us, and that our connection to that power and to one another is grounded in love and compassion.

Practicing spirituality brings a sense of perspective, meaning and purpose to our lives.
Brené Brown

Do It Now Action Point

Look at the four areas of connection and decide which one you want to focus on this week:

      connection to your true self
      connection with a supportive group of people
      connection to a greater purpose
      connection to a higher consciousness

Once you have done that, reflect on the question, "how can I connect more?" For example, how can I connect more to my true self? How can I connect more with the people who truly support me, or, with more supportive people? How can I connect more with my passion purpose? How can I connect more to higher consciousness? You can take your time with this, and practice being open to the Universe showing you answers to your question. I believe inspired action is more effective than forced action. From this reflection identify one or more specific actions you can take this week. Complete one of those actions.

Extra Help

How do I meet new people?
If you need to add some new positive people into your life who will support you as you grow, then joining interest groups can be a good way to meet people. I recommend joining pro-active or activity-based groups rather than problem-based support groups. Sometimes it can help to meet with people who share the same problem as you, but often it can also keep you stuck identifying with that problem. You could try a meditation meet-up, or a small group fitness class, or a creative class of some sort. Building friendships with people who share your passions is very beneficial. Connecting in person is preferable, but sometimes online connections can be helpful as well. Local libraries will usually be able to give you a lot of information about community groups in your area.

I find it hard to trust people
If you feel like connection is an aspect you have room for a lot of growth in, or if you are currently feeling very disconnected in a lot of ways, then your action this week may simply be the reflection process. You may wish to journal your thoughts on the subject, or use it as a focus for meditation. You can reflect on the question of "how can I connect more?" or another option could

be, "what would it take for me to feel safe to connect more?" Remember, if you are really struggling with connecting with other people, then you can use the affirmation statement starter "I want to want . . ." For example:

"I want to want to connect to other people"
"I want to want to trust people"

Traumatic experiences in relationships in the past can cause your survival brain to create fears to keep you safe, but which prevent you from developing positive relationships going forward. You can rewire your brain to overcome these, but it is beyond the scope of this book to teach you how. If you have significant fears and blocks to forming positive healthy relationships, then I recommend seeing a qualified therapist or coach who will be able to help you, as you will not be able to experience full happiness if you have difficulties positively connecting with other people.

Turbo-Boost

Reflect on more than one of the four areas of connection (you can look at all four if you want to), come up with action points, and take one action for each area.

Create Connection Practice Steps

> Reflect on how you can create more connection in one of the four areas, write down some actions you can take to achieve this, and complete one of these actions this week.

> If you have significant issues with connection, then you may wish to simply reflect on the question of

"how can I connect more?" or "what would it take for me to feel safe to connect more?"

> Turbo Boost this step by reflecting on more than one of the four areas of connection (you can look at all four if you want to), come up with action points, and take one action for each area.

What Next?

Well done! You made it to the end! (well, I'm assuming you didn't just skip to the end).

So, what next?

It is likely that there were a number of steps in this book that you haven't fully worked through yet. Therefore, I recommend that you reference back through the book and for each step rate yourself on a scale of 1-10 for how well you think you are practicing the step. Once you have done that, rate the steps in terms of which ones you could improve on the most, or which ones you could work on more that are most important to you. Alternatively, you could start working through all the steps again with the same week by week focus.

If you found the practices in this book helpful, then I do recommend that you stay with it and continue to embed the practices before you move on to something else. Not because I think this book is significantly better than other information available, but because, as I said in the introduction, it is only when knowledge is put into action that you get results. You need to stay with a particular learning long enough for it to become a habit that brings you consistent results, otherwise its value is limited, and it is likely to just contribute to information overwhelm.

You don't need to know it all. You need to know and do things that work effectively for you. When you find that, stay with it, invest in it.

Let go of the fear of missing out on the informational magic pill, and trust that when you treat yourself with love, and make a clear decision about who you want to be and the life you want to live, that your reticular activating system, quantum physics and the creative divine will guide you to all that you need.

Thank you for taking this journey with me.
I would love to receive any feedback you may have about the book. You can post a review online or email info@janinelattimore.com

Wishing you love and happiness
Janine

Appendix: Summary Infographics

On the following pages are a series of graphics that summarise the key concepts of the book.

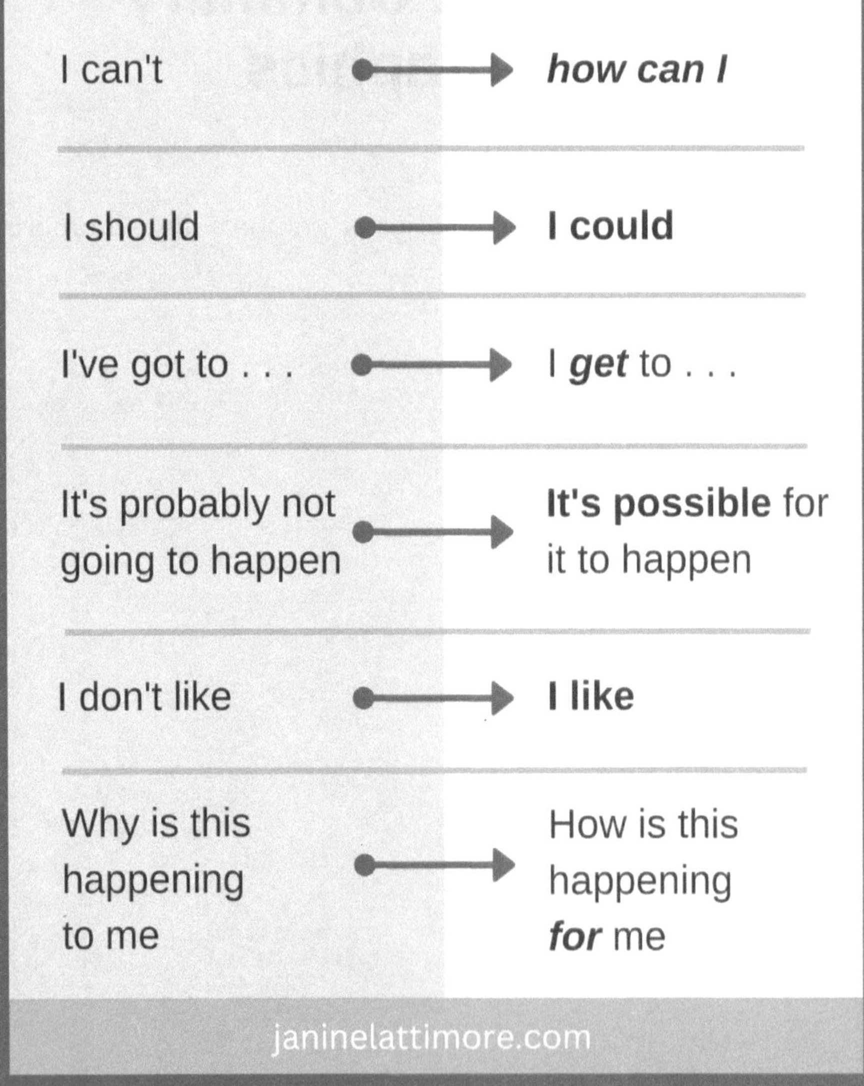
10 STEPS TO HAPPINESS
Empowering Rephrases
I can't
how can I
I should
I could
I've got to . . .
I get to . . .
It's probably not going to happen
It's possible for it to happen
I don't like
I like
Why is this happening to me
How is this happening for me
janinelattimore.com

3 Part Self-love Practice:

Trigger Body Love

Trigger an emotion
present, past, or problem

Feel it in your **body**

I **love** myself for feeling . . .

---

3 Part Belief Deactivation Process:

Recognise, Decide, Focus

RECOGNISE your current beliefs

DECIDE what you want to believe

FOCUS on what you want

How to Fill Your Own Love Bucket

Say the affirmation "I choose to love myself,
just as I am" each time you
look in a mirror

· ·

Appreciate what you have achieved

· ·

Appreciate who you are

· ·

Date yourself

· ·

Ask "what would I do if I truly loved myself"
when making daily decisions

· ·

Reflect on the question: "how am I settling
for less than I deserve or less than is fair?"

janinelattimore.com

Power of 5 Practices

Give yourself a re-start

Sustain pleasure · Move your body

Listen to music · Be in nature

Bin It and Pin It Game · Hug someone/ a pet

Gratitude · Laugh freely

Meditate/Be Present

Trigger Body Love Practice
Talk to Your Fear Bodyguard
Use "What If" Positively

Journaling

Appreciate what you have achieved
Appreciate who you are
How am I settling for less than I deserve?

I Am Enough Affirmation
I Choose to Love Myself As I Am Affirmation

janinelattimore.com

About the Author

Janine Lattimore's three greatest passions since she was very young have been writing, teaching and the health and development of mind, body and soul. She endeavours to live what she learns and teaches, and embraces life as an adventure of experience and expansion.

A mother of two children, over the course of her life so far Janine has worked as a teacher, youth worker, community development worker, cleaner, hula hoop fitness instructor, virtual assistant, Nia teacher and learning assistant. She has been facilitating classes and workshops, and writing about various aspects of wellbeing and personal development since 2004. Janine is certified as an NLP Practitioner and Coach, a Nia somatic movement instructor, and as a VITA Sex, Love and Relationships Coach working through embodiment modalities. Other books authored by her include: *The Great Life Planner*, *How to Make Fear Your Friend*, *How to Attract a Great Partner*, *Creative Hoop Play* and *Free to Eat*, which are all available from Amazon and most online book platforms.

Janine's mission in life is to provide easy to follow, effective pathways for herself and others to decrease suffering and increase fulfilment through creating greater connection, love, and joy in their lives.

You can access more of Janine's work at janinelattimore.com